The Writer's Sourcebook

Also by Rachel Friedman Ballon:

Blueprint for Writing: A Writer's Guide to Creativity, Craft & Career

The Writer's Sourcebook

From Writing Blocks to Writing Blockbusters

by
Rachel Friedman Ballon

LOWELL HOUSE

LOS ANGELES

CONTEMPORARY BOOKS

CHICAGO

Library of Congress Cataloging-in-Publication Data
Ballon, Rachel Friedman.
    The writer's sourcebook : from writing blocks to writing blockbusters /
by Rachel Friedman Ballon.
       p. cm.
    Includes bibliographical references (p.) and index.
    ISBN 1-56565-466-8
    ISBN 1-56565-816-7 (paperback)
    1. Authorship—Handbooks, manuals, etc. I. Title.
PN147.B317 1996
808'.02—dc20
                                     96-31049
                                     CIP

Requests for such permissions should be addressed to:
Lowell House
2020 Avenue of the Stars, Suite 300
Los Angeles, CA 90067

Lowell House books can be purchased at special discounts when ordered in bulk
for premiums and special sales. Contact Department TC at the address above.

Publisher: Jack Artenstein
Associate Publisher, Lowell House Adult: Bud Sperry
Director of Publishing Services: Rena Copperman
Managing Editor: Maria Magallanes
Text design: Nancy Freeborn

Manufactured in the United States of America
10 9 8 7 6 5 4 3 2 1

Acknowledgments

A big thank you to my husband Bill, who always believed in and encouraged my writing. To my two sons, John and Marc, who were always willing to read parts of the manuscript and give wonderful suggestions.

Thanks and appreciation to my editor, Bud Sperry, who brought the idea of a writers sourcebook to me and through his guidance and suggestions encouraged me to create this book.

I want to thank the following for their time and assistance: Steve Fayne, who generously helped with the contract; Carolyn Miller, who gave me resources for the section on interactive writing; Pam Douglas, who shared her valuable information about television episodic dramas; and Brenda Krantz, for her suggestions and sources on playwriting.

To my special friends and colleagues—writers and writing consultants—whose support and suggestions helped make this book diversified and unique. A grateful thank you to Adrienne Fayne, Suzanne Blum, Len Felder, Marjorie Miller, Linda Seger, Naomi Feldman, and Blos Elfman.

And lastly, I am indebted to all my writing clients and students throughout the years, who asked the right questions, allowing me to find the right answers for this book.

This book is dedicated to all the men and women who have a writer locked inside, wanting to come out!

Contents

Introduction

"Writing, like life itself, is a voyage of discovery."
—*Henry Miller*

At one time or another, everybody feels compelled to write. Whether they write personal memoirs, scripts, novels, short stories, children's books, an autobiography, poetry, plays, business articles, greeting cards, sitcoms, or a journal, people want to express themselves through the written word.

Maybe that's why writing is the number-one hobby in the United States. Every day, millions of would-be writers take classes, attend seminars, buy books and tapes, and attend conferences in their pursuit of learning how to write. Many have watched a television show, read a book, and seen a movie and said to themselves, "If I wanted to, I could write something better."

Sounds easy, doesn't it? Well, it's easier said than done. Writing is hard work, and most people who attempt to write the great American novel or the blockbuster script don't know how to get their thoughts down on the page. Others can't get started or, once started, get stuck in the middle. Those few who finish their writing project often ask, What do I do now that I've finished? Who do I sell this to? How can I get some production company to buy my script? How do I get an agent? What publisher will publish my work?

These questions often remain unanswered because writers don't know how to make sense of all this confusion. They haven't learned the ins and outs of the writing business and haven't figured out how to get through the door of this mysterious world. They don't know how to get access to the world of agents, publishers, production companies, editors, booksellers, networks, and the like. They often quit in defeat. Writers who attempt to get their writing out into the world often put it back in the closet when they get rejected, never to try again. It's easy to see why so few become successful in the field of writing.

These questions are the same asked by thousands of writers at the writing workshops I conduct throughout the United States and Canada. In these workshops, I deal with important writing issues of art, craft, and selling.

Once writers—beginners and professionals—complete their writing projects, it's often more difficult for them to find out how to sell their writing than it was for them to write it. The most basic problem writers encounter after they've written their project is figuring out what to do next.

Although there are hundreds of books on the market about how to write, they usually focus on only one aspect of the writing industry—self-publishing, for example, or how to get an agent, or how to sell your articles, or how to write for the children's market, or how to be a free-lance writer. Unfortunately, most publishers haven't put enough diverse information into one sourcebook.

Years ago, when I finished my first full-length script, I had no idea what to do next. It took years of frustration and rejection before a major studio optioned it. It would have been much easier and a lot less time-consuming if I had had knowledge of what to expect, whom to contact, and which movie studio would be interested in my type of script—a romantic-comedy—before I started to market it. It probably wouldn't have taken years to get my project sold if I had had a guidebook containing all the necessary information.

I had to find out most of the information myself, through trial and error. All of the knowledge in this book comes from my own firsthand experiences with getting an agent, dealing with the agent, finding another agent; marketing my writing, getting rejections, selling my writing; taking meetings at studios, getting rejected at studios, getting my scripts produced; self-publishing, marketing, and distributing my own book; and eventually finding the right publisher for my book and learning about contracts and royalties.

From all these experiences, the good, the bad, and the ugly, I have gathered valuable insider's information to impart to each and every one of you. And that is how *The Writer's Sourcebook* came into being.

In 1994 I wrote *Blueprint for Writing: A Writer's Guide to Creativity, Craft & Career* based on my workshops, to teach writers an easy-to-follow step-by-step method for taking ideas and working them through to completed script or manuscript. This book is the one for you if you aren't familiar with the techniques and craft of writing. Think of it as a companion book to the one you're now reading.

The Writer's Sourcebook will not only tell you how to write for the different markets but also help in navigating all aspects of the writing process. It will keep you moving in the right direction until you publish, get a writing job, sell your work, or achieve your writing goal.

The Writer's Sourcebook is personal yet practical. It's creative and career-oriented. It's general yet specific. It deals with prose and procrastination, proposals and publishing, query letters and pitches, seminars and sitcoms, writing workshops and words. It informs you about topics ranging from style to selling, from vision to voice, from conferences to contests, from agents to articles, from formats to features, from getting started to finishing, from making contacts to negotiating contracts, from making deals to making money.

By reading and working *The Writer's Sourcebook*, you will discover everything you ever wanted to know about writing and the writing business. Even if you just want to write for your own enjoyment or to publish but not sell your writing, this book will help you find your niche as a writer. For those of you who do want to sell your work, it will provide practical information on how to make a living as a writer and help you develop strategies to market your writing. It will give you inside information about the writing industry and keep you on target until you reach your goal.

After reading it, you will have more than a fighting chance in a business fraught with more supply than demand, diminishing markets, and fierce competition, with fewer books published and fewer films produced each year.

The Writer's Sourcebook will give you an edge over other writers—both wanna-bes and professionals—in an intensely competitive market. You will come to the marketplace prepared and empowered.

Through reading *The Writer's Sourcebook*, you'll learn how to target your writing with an understanding of what the other side is looking for, which will afford you a better opportunity to publish your work.

The Writer's Sourcebook will tell you everything you need to know about the inner workings and the outer realities of the writing game. It will teach you what the rules of the business are. By learning the rules, you'll become a more savvy writer.

Let *The Writer's Sourcebook* demystify the world of writing for you. Keep it by your side during the writing process. Refer to it as you develop your action plan for writing, targeting, and selling your finished product.

With this sourcebook as your companion, you'll never lose your direction in your journey to success. This book will allow you to stay on the right course until you reach your goal.

CHAPTER ONE

The Writer's Path: From Getting Ready to Getting Started

"If you want to become a writer, it is very necessary to expose yourself to the vicissitudes of life."

—*W. Somerset Maugham*

Why Do You Want to Write?

People have many reasons for wanting to write. Some want their thoughts, ideas, and philosophies revealed through the written word. Others want to make millions writing a best-seller. Still others love the sound of words and the rhythm of metaphors, similes, and imagery.

There are people who live to write and others who write to live. However, the majority of writers fall somewhere in between these two extremes—writers who just want to write for fun, and those who want to see their writing in print.

Whether you are an experienced writer or have never written before, there are certain traits you need to have to write successfully. Aside from an active imagination, creativity, and an inquiring mind, you also must have the courage to reveal who you are through the written word.

Here's an exercise: Take a moment to get quiet with yourself, close your eyes, and take a few deep breaths. After a few minutes, answer the question "Why do I want to write?" The answer will come to you as you take your pen and write as fast as you can for twenty minutes without worrying about grammar, punctuation, or spelling. Keep writing until the twenty minutes are up, and above all, don't stop.

When you've finished, read over what you have written. Does it reveal to you the real reasons you want to write? Are your reasons strong enough to keep you going when you become frustrated, blocked, or rejected? It's important for you to know and understand your motivation for writing. If it comes from within you, you will probably write no matter what.

Every day, new writers join the millions of existing ones, but many soon fall by the wayside. Others become successful and are rewarded with money, fame, and a sense of accomplishment. Your choices for writing are as unlimited as the choices you make for your ideas. It doesn't matter what the form or genre, what does matter is that you express yourself and your ideas with the best possible writing. The most successful writers aren't necessarily the most talented or creative ones. They are the writers who don't quit. They perfect their craft by consistently putting in the hours and the hard work. Above all, they have the courage to persevere and stay motivated, even when their writing is rejected, because they believe in themselves and their writing.

These writers are motivated internally. They don't write because their family, friends, or other writers like what they have written. And they don't stop because others criticize their work. Eventually they succeed in their writing endeavor, reaping the rewards and the satisfaction of successfully completing and selling their work.

Isn't that what most successful people in any field do? They work hard, persevere, and believe in themselves. Successful people need these qualities whether they're in business, law, medicine, or any other venture.

The following is a list of thirteen qualities that I believe are necessary to be a successful writer:

Thirteen Character Traits for Writing Success

1. **FLEXIBILITY.** Being flexible means being resilient and able to make changes in your work. It means listening to others' criticism and doing what you have to do without being hardheaded. The ability to revise, rewrite and do whatever you have to do, to make your story work, even if you have to rewrite your story over and over. It is the opposite of being rigid and closed-off to new ideas.

2. **CREATIVITY.** Your imagination is a wonderful gift. Are you able to daydream? Writing down your fantasies is the first step to getting your ideas and concepts from your fertile inner creative source down on paper.

3. **MOTIVATION.** Your desire to be a writer must come from inside you. Don't write because other people praise you or think you should be a writer. It is this inner motivation that keeps you going after your writing has been rejected.

4. **PERSEVERANCE.** This is one of the most important ingredients for writing success. If you give up in the face of rejection and disappointment, how will you ever succeed? Perseverance is a quality of all successful writers.

5. **SPONTANEITY.** When you begin writing, you need the ability to be spontaneous without analyzing or criticizing the writing too soon in the process. The first time you write, you want to just get the story down, without editing or rewriting; otherwise, you'll never finish anything.

6. **COURAGE.** It also takes courage to put your feelings on the page and reveal yourself to yourself as well as to others and to keep going in the face of rejection.

7. **FOCUS.** A writer must be able to focus his attention on the work in front of him, even when it's not going well.

8. **REALISTIC.** Being realistic in your writing goals is as important as being able to write. You will get discouraged if you aren't realistic about your chances for success. You have to be shrewd to sell your product in an industry where supply exceeds demand.

9. **VISION.** What is your vision for your writing? What's the point of writing without having something you want to share with the universe? You are only as limited as your thinking. Open yourself and your writing to new ideas and allow your characters to behave in new ways.

10. **PASSION.** Who wants to read lifeless and bland writing? Nobody. Bring your passions and your power to your writing to make it come alive. Whatever you write, remain enthusiastic and passionate about it, even when it's not going well. Your passion for your project will keep you writing whenever you become discouraged. Passion gives you the energy you need to stay on your writing journey.

11. **OBJECTIVITY.** After you've completed your first draft, you need to be objective and study your writing from a practical and objective point of view. Study your writing as if you were an editor, and read it with a critical eye.

12. **COMMUNICATION.** Are you able to communicate with clarity and passion what it is you want to say to your audience?

13. **DISCIPLINE.** Although everyone would like to avoid talking about it, discipline is one of the most important characteristics for a writer to have. It takes discipline to continue writing day after day without knowing if your writing will be published or sold. Discipline enables you to take your ideas and turn them into a cohesive article, book, or script. It takes discipline to develop a schedule for your writing and stick to it, no matter what.

You don't need to have all of these qualities to write, but developing them will make the journey easier.

No matter what your reasons for writing, by the end of this book you'll have all the information you need to fulfill your dream of being a writer.

CHAPTER TWO

What Do You Want to Write?

"Better by far to write twaddle or anything, anything, than nothing at all."

—Katherine Mansfield

The next step in your journey is to choose a specific type of writing. Spend some time thinking about your personality by answering the following questions:

- Are you an introvert or an extrovert?
- Should you write with a partner or alone?
- What types of books or films are you attracted to?
- Are you a fan of nonfiction rather than fiction?
- Do you love to read biographies or historical novels?
- Do visual images excite you more than the written word?
- Are you interested in Gothic novels, romance novels, or mainstream novels?
- Do you enjoy mysteries?
- Are you partial to whodunits or thrillers?
- Would you like to write light, humorous stories?
- Do you have a sense of drama that lends itself to serious dramatic writing?

- Do you watch films and television but almost never read a book?

- Do you like small, personal films or larger-than-life action-adventures?

- Are you intrigued by television soaps or sitcoms?

- Do you like television movies, hospital dramas, or police stories?

These questions are designed to help you choose the type of writing you want to do. It's important for you to take stock of your reading and viewing likes and dislikes before you decide what you want to write. It would be unproductive to start writing a romance novel if you've never read one. It would be a waste of effort to write a television sitcom without ever having watched one.

Often, writers look down their noses at the programs on television, then try to write a sitcom. Not surprisingly, it doesn't work, because you can't write for programs that you don't enjoy.

Be sure you respect the genre you're writing for or you won't give it the effort it deserves. Find out what you love and then target your writing accordingly.

If you still can't decide what you want to write, list your passions, your loves, your hates, your vision, and your view of the world. Think about your interests, beliefs, and values. Through what medium would you like to express them? Do your ideas seem to lend themselves to film or fiction? To nonfiction or a television drama? To a magazine or newspaper article?

If you write long descriptions using flowery words, you're probably better off writing prose than scripts. If you like sentences with little or no description and lots of dialogue, you're probably better off writing scripts. Study your likes and dislikes, and you'll eventually discover what type of writing you want to do. You will learn that content often dictates form.

However, if you're still unsure of what to write, make a list of the following:

- Your five favorite sitcoms
- Your five favorite movies
- Your five favorite novels
- Your five favorite magazines
- Your five favorite authors
- Your five favorite short stories

Identifying your favorite authors and films will help you gravitate toward the type of writing you want to do.

But maybe you don't like fiction at all and are attracted to nonfiction articles about politics, commerce, economics, history, music, or science. Then you will probably want to write for newspapers or magazines. Many nonfiction writers focus on their special interests and develop an area of expertise.

One gentleman, a well-known movie critic, first worked as a reporter for a local paper. In his free time, he wrote free-lance articles about the entertainment industry and sent them to magazines and newspapers. He created a niche for his writing with his passion for films and television. Eventually, he was hired as a movie and TV critic with a well-known publication. Today his reviews and interviews appear on national television programs about the entertainment industry, and all because he followed his bliss!

A former writing student of mine used her vocation as a nutritionist to write articles on health and diet for different magazines. The articles expanded into a book, and she became an expert in low-fat diets and recipes. And another writer incorporated his love of travel into writing about exotic people and places. Through his articles, he provided readers with travel tips and information. Soon his articles began to pay for his traveling expenses.

Finding your niche as a writer will be an exciting process. Whatever type of writing you choose will be just fine, as long as your writing style is consistent with that genre. You must familiarize yourself with the genre you choose *before* you begin to write, by reading books or seeing plays or viewing films. Also diversify, and don't limit yourself to just one writing category.

Many students in my script-writing classes earn their living as newspaper reporters or technical, corporate, public relations, or promotional writers. Some work as advertising copywriters. Even though they earn their livelihood through writing, they still want to write their personal novel or screenplay from the heart rather than from the head. They want to share what's inside their soul and write about what's important to them rather than writing about products, services, or people.

When Do You Want to Write?

"I never write when I'm drunk."

—*W.H. Auden*

There is no right time for writing. You might like to write when everyone in your house is asleep. Or you might write whenever you have fifteen minutes to spare during your busy day. When you write is a personal and practical decision that depends on your life and your needs. So don't compare yourself to anyone else.

There are writers who have a tough time getting themselves to the computer and find a hundred excuses not to write. Others live to write and have nothing else in their lives. How much time you put into your writing might depend on several factors:

- Do you want to make a living as a writer?

- Do you want to write only part-time?

- Are you willing to take a job as a waitress, taxi driver, receptionist, or personal trainer to support yourself until you sell your writing?
- Do you want to write early in the morning or late at night before going to bed?

Obviously, if you want to be a professional writer, you will have to schedule the time to fulfill your writing goals.

If you're going to make writing a part of your life, then you have to develop a plan. To do this, you must understand yourself and your personality. Are you a night person, never going to sleep until the wee hours? Or do you jump out of bed at five o'clock in the morning? Can you concentrate for long periods of time, or do you have to break up your writing schedule because you become easily distracted?

The point is that you have to know your habits and your body's rhythms. So answer the following questions to find out when you should write:

- Do you like working with a schedule?
- Are you disciplined and able to work on your own?
- Do you need outside deadlines and assignments to keep you going?
- Are you spontaneous, only working when the spirit moves you?

There are no right or wrong answers, no better or worse way to write. The point is to *know* yourself, to listen to your internal needs, and to work around your personal habits.

If you can't seem to motivate yourself, set some specific daily goals. For example, you can set a goal to write one page a day, and in one month you'll have written thirty pages. Set reachable goals, so you won't become discouraged or overwhelmed by looking at the entire project. If you tend to procrastinate, make a pact with yourself or a friend that you won't watch television or read until you've completed your writing. Setting up goals and making a commitment to someone else is a helpful way to keep writing when you feel resistant.

Now that you've determined what you want to write and when you want to write, it's time to get started.

CHAPTER THREE

Getting Started: From Printers to Pens

"The beginning is half of any action."

—*Greek proverb*

Many would-be writers have wonderful ideas, great life experiences and decide they want to write about them. So they spend a fortune on the latest high-tech computer and software programs, colored monitors, modems, CD ROM and then sit down to write and wonder why the words aren't flowing. Before long, they put their ideas in the closet along with the computer and forget all about writing. Let's see why this is such a common occurrence.

To be a writer you first must learn the craft of writing BEFORE you write your short story, your novel, your screenplay, or your children's book. Would you ever try to drive a car without some knowledge of the instruments? Of course you wouldn't. Yet most people mistakenly believe that if they can write a letter or a term paper, they know the rudiments of writing. They soon discover it's not quite that easy.

To understand the craft of writing is to understand plot, character development, conflict, resolution, climax, crisis, theme, dialogue, subtext, obstacles, and denouement, among other elements.

In the next chapter I will discuss craft, so for now let's concentrate on getting started.

To avoid getting stuck, understand that your writing doesn't have to be perfect—and it certainly isn't going to be. Just put your ideas down on the page and let the words tumble out. That is the way you get started. You get started by starting. As I tell everyone when they begin a project, it doesn't have to be right; just write it.

When you get your idea, write it down as fast as you can, before it evaporates. Then you can start dealing with craft, characterization, and structure. But if you start worrying about craft at the beginning and don't write anything until you think it's perfect, you'll end up with nothing but a blank page.

It doesn't matter how you write when you start, because you'll eventually have to rewrite it anyway, to include all the elements that make a good story. If you start to worry about all these techniques *before* you begin writing, you'll be overwhelmed and discouraged, and you'll eventually quit.

> "No professional writer can afford only to write when he feels like it."
>
> —*W. Somerset Maugham*

Stop talking about your ideas, analyzing them, worrying about them, thinking about them. Just write them down on the page in black and white any way you can. At this initial stage, don't worry about anything else but putting pen to page or fingers to keyboard. Get your idea down, and remember it doesn't have to be perfect. It doesn't even have to be all that good.

You can't make it better if you don't have any words written down, can you? Continue to get your thoughts from your head to the paper until you've finished your first draft. That's when the real writing begins. You'll then deal with how to use the rules of your craft to organize your writing into a professional piece. Then you'll continue rewriting, editing, and improving your work until you're satisfied that you've given it your best effort.

Writing starts with you. To be a writer includes a sense of language, a love of words, a respect for ideas, and a knowledge of the human condition. There can be no writing without you. You are the characters. You are the stories. Accept yourself and write your truth. You need to have a belief not only in yourself but also in your ideas and your dreams.

Good writing takes preparation, a plan, and hard work. As a writer who wants to improve your craft, you need to be familiar with the tools of the trade. Just as a pianist needs a piano and a figure skater needs ice skates, a writer must have the proper tools. If you want to start writing on a yellow pad or notebook, that is just fine, but the final product must be typewritten in the proper format. Don't ever send a handwritten manuscript to an agent, a publisher, an editor, or a producer. It's totally unprofessional.

You'll need either a good typewriter or a computer. If you don't know how to type, hire a typist. Look in your local Yellow Pages for a listing of typists who are competent with word processing, because then you can have your manuscript on a disk. Today, many publishers ask for a computer disk in addition to a manuscript.

Have an up-to-date dictionary by your side, as well as a thesaurus and a set of encyclopedias. If you have a computer, it will probably have a thesaurus and a spell check. You absolutely cannot send out your writing with misspelled words, because that is the mark of an amateur.

It's also good to have a rhyming dictionary if you're writing poetry. Go to the reference section of your local library and see what other books would be helpful tools for you to have by your side when you write.

The Elements of Style, by William Strunk and E.B. White, is a must for every writer, stressing grammar and explaining various writing styles.

William Zinnser's On Writing Well and Writing to Learn are excellent books on the basic principles of writing. Keep them by your side when you write.

I like to have quotations from other writers on hand when I write. Quotes help me focus what I want to say or affirm a point I want to make. *Bartlett's Familiar Quotations,* published by Little, Brown & Company, contains hundreds of sayings from public figures.

Research

No matter what you write, even if it's a fairy tale or fantasy, you must be accurate and do your research. The saying "Write what you know" doesn't always apply. The quote should go on to say, "Research what you don't know and then write it."

If you could only write what you know, there would be no historical novels, murder mysteries, science fiction, fantasy, or thrillers. These types of novels must be researched to ring true. If you are writing a nonfiction article or book, you must research your facts. I remember writing an article about living alone and having to do tons of research on the demographics of single people.

To me, the saying "Write what you know" refers to your emotional life experiences. What you felt like being in love, burying a loved one, getting married, being ill, moving away, saying goodbye. If you've never been to China and want to set your novel there, you can research the country, the people, the culture, and the economy until you have an accurate setting.

When I tell most writers to write what they know, I'm referring to their passions, their truths, and their feelings. Don't limit your creativity or imagination, but be willing to do the necessary research on your subject.

If you want to write a script about World War I or a science-fiction novel about outer space, you must do your research. Remember that someone has knowledge or experience about whatever you write. Don't take shortcuts. Do your research at the local library, through old newspapers, or the Internet.

Research your setting, your history, your dates, and the atmosphere and general trends of the period you're writing about. Research, research, research, and know when enough is enough. At some point, you have to stop researching and write your story. Don't use research as an excuse not to write, and don't get bogged down with research. *Get on with the story.* You can always go back and do more research.

Writing with a Computer

"Forming a new habit is like winding string on a ball."

—*William James*

The computer has done as much for writing as the automobile did for traveling. For those of you who don't have a computer, I suggest you buy one. A computer can increase your output and your productivity. It's a terrific advantage to be able to correct mistakes without having to retype a whole page or even an entire scene. Computers allow you to correct all the errors you make in a matter of seconds. No tedious and laborious rewriting, no correction tapes, and no messy correction fluid to deal with. With a computer, you can take passages from the middle of your work and move them to the beginning. You can delete entire chapters without destroying your overall structure. You have the freedom to move sections of your piece around, cutting and pasting without scissors or paste. You can also format your manuscript to have any size margins or change the fonts and the type style before you print it out.

Unless you want to go back to the good old days of the horse and buggy, I suggest you invest in a computer at some point in your writing career.

My own output doubled when I bought my first computer. I give my computer all the credit. When my editor gave me notes on changes he wanted incorporated, when I rewrote *Blueprint for Writing*, I literally was able to change text, move words, paragraphs, or pages around. I deleted and inserted text wherever I had to, without redoing the entire book. Rewriting was a much more pleasant and productive process than it was when I wrote without a computer. I didn't have to spend weeks or even months reworking the book.

Nowadays, a computer is much more than a word-processing tool. It is also a means of accessing information, without ever leaving your home or office. With the advent of the Internet and the World Wide Web, you can find more material than you could ever imagine. All you have to do is join one of the online services, like CompuServe, America On-Line, or Prodigy, and you are able to connect to a vast network called the World Wide Web.

Would you be satisfied if your local newspaper was your only source of information? Of course not. Well, that is what it's like not to have a computer. The Internet gives you access to national and international research at libraries, universities, and data banks. A computer gives you a myriad of opportunities to exchange information with other writers as well.

You probably can't even imagine what your life would be like without the telephone, the television, or the airplane, because you take those conveniences for granted. Well, the same will eventually hold true for computers and the Internet.

If you're worried about not understanding computers, there are many good books you can turn to, especially the "Dummy" series published by IDG Books—*Mac for Dummies, MS Word for Dummies, Windows 95 for Dummies,* to name a few. If you don't want to lay out the money for these books, go to your local library and read up on the various computers and computer products available before you make your purchase.

It took me over a year to find the right store to help me purchase a computer to fit my needs. I didn't even know what questions to ask.

Don't buy a computer from a cut-rate chain if the sales clerks don't help you understand what your needs are. Computer training is offered at community colleges, through university extension programs, and by individual consultants. Some computer stores offer in-store training with your purchase. Sometimes these classes are included in the purchase price, but in most cases there is an extra charge for training. It's well worth it. Don't be penny wise and pound foolish and have your computer end up in the shipping crate. What's the point of having a computer if you don't know how to use it?

The main computer operating systems are Macintosh and MS DOS or MS Windows. Try the different systems before you buy, and see which one fits most of your needs. After you choose a computer, you need to have software for it. (Think of a computer as a CD player and the software program as the CD.)

Nowadays you might want to get a computer with a fax modem and CD-ROM. Some popular brands of computers are Compaq, Hewlett Packard, IBM, Apple, Toshiba, Epson, AST, NEC, Digital, and Packard Bell.

It is extremely important when using a computer to "save" your work, throughout your writing. Do not wait until you've finished. If you don't periodically save it onto a disk, you might lose the entire document and be left empty-handed. Believe me, that has happened to me after I've worked hours on a project. One way this might happen is through a malfunction of your computer system, or a power failure. So be diligent and back up your work as you go along.

Computer Software Programs for Writers

When you buy software, be sure it's compatible with your particular computer. So many writers bought Windows 95 only to discover that their computer didn't have enough memory to operate it.

Many software companies have customer service numbers

you can call for support. Some companies have 800 numbers, and others don't. It can get quite expensive while you're hanging on the line, listening to piped-in music and paying for a long-distance call. Check out the support for your computer and your software program and see if it suits your needs and your pocketbook.

The following are some of the software programs that are designed to aid writers:

- WritePro (Mac & IBM)

- Dramatica (Mac & IBM)

- Writer's Blocks (IBM)

- Three by Five (Mac)

- Storyline (Mac & IBM)

- Plots Unlimited (Mac & IBM)

Printers

If you're planning to submit your writing to publishers or production companies, it's important to get a letter-quality printer—meaning the letters are sharp and clear and easy to read.

Dot matrix printers used to be fuzzy, but now they are almost letter quality. However, I urge you to send out manuscripts that are only letter quality, because publishers don't want to read dot-matrix manuscripts. (They end up seeing dots before their eyes.)

Buy a laser or an ink-jet printer. Your writing will look professional and be very readable. Some popular brands are Hewlett Packard, Epson, Packard Bell, and Macintosh. Canon makes a line of portable bubble jet printers that are reliable, lightweight, and compact.

Computer Stores Specializing in Serving Writers

The Writer's Computer Store
11317 Santa Monica Boulevard
Los Angeles, California 90025
(310) 479-7774

The Writer's Computer Store
2631 Bridgeway Avenue
Sausalito, California 94965
(415) 332-7005

These stores specialize in all types of computers and software programs for writers. They do mail-order business throughout the United States and Canada. To inquire about their mail-order service, call (800) 272-8927.

Pens and Paper

I know many writers who are compulsive pen and notebook buyers, myself included. I can spend weeks or months searching for the perfect notebook. And when I see someone writing with a well-made pen, I'll ask him where he bought it and track it down with the zeal of a detective.

Pens and paper are very personal materials for writers. I've seen writers use notebooks so tiny, it's unbelievable that they can decipher their writing. I've seen other writers cover only one side of each sheet in a large notebook before going to the next page.

Many writers like to use a pen and paper to get the story down, then switch to a computer or typewriter. I like to write the first draft or at least the ideas down on paper. There are several reasons for this. First, I always carry my notebook with me, since the germination of an idea for a screenplay or a book often takes time. So I make constant notes in my notebook, and it helps me work on the idea until it forms some sort of a story.

I could probably accomplish the same thing working on a computer, but my preference is to write in longhand first. Somehow it seems more personal, with feelings coming from my hand through the pen onto the page.

Speaking of pens, I prefer a black pen for writing and a red or green pen for editing. I like pens that can write as fast as I think up my story, and I've found that a roller-ball pen is my preference. I've been through them all: Pentel's Rolling Writer, Entre's Super Roller, Pentel's Rock n' Write, Pilot's Ball Liner, Uniball's Onyx, Uniball's Deluxe, Bic's Roller, and Pilot's Precise V7 fine.

Many of you might like writing with a fountain pen, from an inexpensive Schaffer to the extravagant Monte Blanc. Whatever your preference, it's important to find the pen that's just right for you, the perfect pen with which to write your precious stories, poems, or articles. Writing with a pen you enjoy somehow makes the writing flow.

Recently, I was having lunch with a fellow writer and we were discussing our mutual projects. I asked her what type of pen she used, and she pulled out a bunch of ballpoint pens that sell for something like one dollar for a dozen. I was shocked that she didn't have a more special pen and told her so. I reached into my briefcase and pulled out an assortment of ten or more different pens and urged her to try each one. She did and liked them all. Although she said the ballpoint pen she had was satisfactory and that a pen didn't matter to her, a couple of months later I saw her using one of the pens I had introduced her to.

When I asked her why she was using it, she laughed. "You've cost me more money, because after I tried your pen, I bought one and got hooked," she said. "It now costs me over fourteen dollars more for a dozen of these pens."

She then told me about her daughter, an exchange student in Spain, who also became hooked on the pen. She called her mother from Spain, requesting she send two dozen pens.

Experiment with different pens, and when you like the flow and the look of the pen and the way it feels in your hand, buy it.

Your choice of notebooks is just as important. I have tried every type of notebook on the market and have my own special requirement. I like a notebook that lies flat when you open it while writing at a café or in a park. A wide-ruled notebook is my favorite—one that has a hard back, so I can use it without a desk or a table.

I've recently found a notebook that has a decorative paper cover and a sturdy back. It even has wide spiral loops, large enough to accommodate my favorite pen, though the notebook is small enough to fit in my purse. You'll see the importance of the right pen and notebook when you look forward to using both every time you write.

CHAPTER FOUR

Telling the Story:
From Structure to Conflict

"True ease in writing comes from art, not chance."

—Alexander Pope

Whether you've chosen to write a novel, a nonfiction book, or a screenplay, you have to know how to tell a good story. You might have a terrific idea and exciting characters, but if you don't know how to build your story in a cohesive structure that will keep your reader or viewer interested, you will have failed.

This chapter is for those of you who not only want to write but also want to master the craft of storytelling. It is for those of you who desire to become professional writers. The *how* of writing is the craft. To have a career in writing, you must learn the rules of writing. After you understand the rules, then you must incorporate them into your writing.

Writing is a contact sport, a hands-on learning experience. Would you try to play a sport as a professional before learning the rules? Of course you wouldn't. Unfortunately, many people believe they can write professionally without learning the rudiments of writing. They soon discover that's not the case.

Writing is a two-part process. The more you write, the more you learn; the more you learn, the better you write. If you don't put the rules into practice, your writing won't improve.

A writer who knows his craft is able to finish each chapter with the reader asking, "What's going to happen next?" To get the reader to keep reading is the ultimate purpose of your craft.

If you can accomplish this in whatever you write, your writing will be interesting and successful. After you've mastered the craft, your finished product will be clear, exciting, and marketable.

The Story Line or Structure

"If I didn't know the ending of a story, I wouldn't begin. I always write my last line, my last paragraph, my last page first."

—*Katherine Ann Porter*

All writers must be able to write a story with a beginning, a middle, and an end. The beginning of the story must relate to the end. Without this relationship, there is no story line or plot. By having an idea of how your story will end, you'll have a better chance of finishing your writing without getting stuck in the middle.

When I teach workshops in structure, I always ask the class if the following examples are plots:

Jack dies and Jill dies. Most of my students say that isn't a plot, just a statement of fact.

Jack dies and Jill dies of a broken heart. Almost everyone agrees that this is a plot, because the actions are related to each other. The beginning relates to the end. Do you understand the difference? In the first example, there is no connection between Jack's death and Jill's death. They might not have even known each other, and the deaths could have occurred years apart.

However, in the second example, Jack dies, and because of his death, Jill also dies from a broken heart. Jack's death leads to Jill's demise. There is an emotional connection between the two characters. The beginning relates to the end and sets off the story line. That is what a plot is—events that are connected from the opening through to the end, and without it, you have nothing.

Laying out any story line is the most difficult part of writing. Unfortunately, many writers only know the opening sentence, and many just visualize a setting or a scene when they begin. Some writers never work from an outline or a plan. They just let their characters take them where they want to go. And do you know where they usually end up? Stuck at a dead end.

Plot, character development, conflict, resolution, climax, crisis, theme, dialogue, subtext, obstacles, and denouement are the elements that make up the structure of your story. Structure is what keeps your story from collapsing. It is the spine of any story, and it allows you to take your idea to completion.

Whether you're writing fiction or nonfiction, articles or books, you must develop a structure for your writing to adhere to so it won't fall apart. In a television script or a screenplay, there is one main story line and usually one or more subplots. The subplots are secondary to the main plot. If they are well-written, they will connect to the main plot, at the end. Being able to connect everything to the main plot line takes great skill.

Casual Writing

"I always have at the very start a curiously clear preview of the entire novel before me or above me."

—*Vladimir Nabokov*

In order to write well-structured stories, in which one problem is built upon the preceding one until everything comes to a successful conclusion, you need to master the art of causal writing. In today's market, you can't bring in a Greek chorus to wrap up your story. The ending has to be motivated by the characters, and the solution must be inherent within the story.

Events must arise through cause and effect and must not be

contrived or happen by accident. In causal writing, your ideas must be related to one another. Think of the scenes in your script or play and the chapters in your novel as pieces of a giant jigsaw puzzle. When you connect all of the pieces, you can see the whole picture. In causal writing, one scene should cause the scene that follows it and evolve from the scene that preceded it.

Causal writing applies to fiction, nonfiction, script writing and play writing. Every chapter in a book and every scene in a script becomes a part of the whole and must relate to the overall story line.

The biggest problem I've seen with both beginners and professional writers is that their scripts or manuscripts are not written in a causal manner. This means that the scenes or chapters don't connect, and they haven't developed a blueprint to hold the structure together. The scenes just occur without any purpose, and the story breaks down.

Since the scenes and chapters build upon one another to form the plot, if you remove one of them your entire structure should collapse. If removing a scene doesn't affect your overall story, then the scene is probably not necessary and should be eliminated. Only include those scenes that relate to your story line.

Comic Relief

It is a good idea to pace your scenes—that is, to follow a strong emotional scene with a quiet scene. An action scene should be preceded by a slower-paced scene. Quiet scenes can be very powerful. They can be moments of introspection, when a character discovers something about himself or another character. Remember the value of comic relief. When things get too heavy, you can use your humor and sensitivity as a writer to pace your scenes throughout your story by interspersing humor with drama.

Premise

You must be able to tell what your story is about in a couple of sentences. This is known as your premise. Think of the premise as a log line in the *TV Guide*. It states in a couple of sentences what the story is about. All scenes you write need to relate to this premise. Ask yourself if the scene helps move your story to its conclusion, and if it does, keep it. But if it doesn't relate to your premise, remove it. All scenes must lead to the climax of your story and its resolution.

Climax or Plot Resolution

> "The last thing we decide in writing a book is what to put first."
>
> —*Blaise Pascal*

Writing is about emotional conflict, and we write stories in which characters have personal problems, thwarted dreams, and passionate goals. We hope that by the end of a story, the characters have solved their problems and realized their dreams. We certainly aren't interested in stories that have no resolution. After all, we can experience that in real life—working in dead-end jobs, being in never-ending relationships, and living lives of quiet desperation.

When we read a book or view a film or a television movie, we want to escape, to see human beings who overcome the odds, who beat the system and conquer the forces of evil. This is what writing is all about. That is why people pay for books and movie tickets.

By the end of the story, your readers and viewers want to experience a resolution to the conflicts. This is the point of all writing, to create a problem in the beginning of your story and to resolve it by the end.

In the climax, the following three elements must happen:

1. The plot must be resolved.

2. The theme must be revealed.

3. The main character must experience a transformation.

Denouement

After the climax you may write a scene that is known as the tag, or the denouemment. The denouement is like tying up the story in a neat package with a bright red ribbon. It is the "and then they lived happily ever after." In a detective story, the denouement comes after the case has been solved and you see the detectives congratulating each other. A denouement gives closure to the entire script and satisfies the audience's need for a resolution.

Anticlimax

When the climax is over, your story is over. Nothing else can happen. If you continue your script after the climax, it will be considered anticlimactic. You'll be left with a weak ending and a dissatisfied audience.

Upping the Stakes

Upping the stakes means giving characters a goal they desperately want, then putting obstacles in their path, preventing them from attaining the goal. Whenever you write, you want to up the stakes, because it creates tension, suspense, and conflict.

Let's take a character whose goal is to keep his position as vice president of marketing in a company that is having major cutbacks and layoffs. He belongs to a country club, owns a home in the suburbs, has three children in college and one in private school, and is carrying a second mortgage on his home. He has been robbing Peter to pay Paul and barely can make the monthly overhead. Now he learns that the company is downsizing. He's upset because he has had to let his longtime assistant go and has watched some of his colleagues be dismissed.

He is fifty-four and has been employed by the ADC Corporation for the past thirty years. He can't sleep nights, and his stress level is high, causing him to get a prescription for tranquilizers. His doctor takes a blood test and finds out he's also suffering from high cholesterol and a high sugar count. He doesn't say anything to his wife and keeps working hard—staying late and driving in early to work. The tension is mounting.

Suppose the executive's wife becomes very ill. Now he needs to keep his job more than ever. He is more desperate. We are more involved. We care about his plight and his family. Will he keep his job? Will his wife's condition worsen? What will he do in response to these pressures? Will he take more pills? Will he turn to alcohol? Will he have a heart attack? By upping the stakes in such ways, you can make your script or novel fast-moving and exciting.

The Time Lock

Characters are revealed under stress or pressure. The more desperately your main character wants to reach a specific goal, the more exciting your story. Put your characters in a pressure cooker and watch how they act and react. One of the best ways of giving your characters intense pressure is to use a "time lock." Put a time limit on the action your character takes and you'll have more suspense in your story and more tension.

For example, a character must discover a bomb that is about to go off in twenty minutes. You are putting a time lock on the situation. This is certainly more exciting than a bomb that will detonate in a week or a month. When you write, put your main character in a situation where he has a limited time to reach his goal. The less time involved, the greater the tension.

You can't see inside a kettle to know the exact moment when the water turns to steam, but it surely will do so when enough heat and pressure build up. Keep the pressure on your characters and you'll keep people interested in your story.

Conflict

Conflict is a major building block of powerful, exciting writing. All writing must contain conflict, but how do you get it? You first give your main character a goal, and then you put obstacles in her path. These obstacles are necessary to create conflict.

All scenes or chapters must have conflict, because without it, you don't have dramatic action. The conflict doesn't have to consist of battles, fights, or wars. It should involve emotional conflict between characters.

If a character doesn't have to struggle, there is no conflict, and without conflict, there is no drama. Conflict adds tension and suspense to your story. The greater the obstacles, the greater the conflict.

Emotional conflict in relationships between people makes the most powerful stories. Stories that involve personal struggles have the most impact. Stories about families and friends touch our hearts, especially those stories that deal with the powerful emotions of love, hate, joy, sorrow, anger, jealousy, and fear. Great films and novels are created from such stories.

As you start to write, take the emotions buried inside you and express them through your characters. By creating characters that are human, frailties and all, your writing will emotionally involve your readers or viewers. There are three types of conflict:

1. Man against man

2. Man against nature

3. Man against himself

Try to have all three types in each of your stories and you will be certain to write exciting work.

The most popular type of conflict involves man against man. The main character has a goal, and another character stands in his way. This type of conflict occurs in most mystery, spy, and war stories. However, the most dramatic form of it is the small, personal story involving families, lovers, or another important emotional relationship. This type includes the movies: *The Piano, Leaving Las Vegas,* and *Muriel's Wedding.*

In all good writing, the main characters should have internal conflict. The best stories are those that include all three types of conflict simultaneously. A story that is personal and contains all three types of conflict makes your writing both dramatic and original.

Dialogue

You never use dialogue just because you want your characters to speak. When you write dialogue, it needs to accomplish one of three things:

1. Give information
2. Move your story forward
3. Reveal character

If your dialogue doesn't fit into any of these categories, don't use it! Never write dialogue just for the sake of small talk. Pleasantries such as "How are you?" and "I'm fine" are boring and will slow down your story. All dialogue must have a purpose, and there is no purpose for small talk.

Avoid adjectives and adverbs like *happily, sadly, angrily,* and *fearfully,* except when your intention might otherwise be unclear. Use crisp dialogue, and pace your short speeches with longer speeches. Intersperse conversations with interruptions and pauses to add variety.

Silence can have more emotional impact than loud conversations. In real life, we communicate nonverbally, through facial expressions and body language, much more than we do when we speak.

When writing dialogue, be aware of your character's tone of voice, facial expression, and eye contact. Close your eyes and imagine what emotion he or she is feeling before you write the dialogue. Instead of using words to communicate your character's feelings, use a gesture, a facial expression, or body movement.

Common Mistakes When Writing Dialogue

The most common mistake when writing diologue is to make all the characters sound the same. This problem occurs when writers only write from one voice and are afraid to reach inside to connect to all their different voices.

The next most common problem with dialogue is not having any differentiation between the characters' styles of speech. So the dialogue sounds the same.

Before you write dialogue, get inside your characters and listen to them talk. If a character is a teenager in the 1990s, she'll sound different from a teenager in the 1930s. Decide what type of speech is appropriate, depending on whether the character is a society matron, a waitress, a gangster, a teenager, educated, illiterate, rural, or urban.

The second most common mistake when writing dialogue is writing monologues or long-winded speeches. In dialogue, less is more. Avoid meaningless chitchat, and make each word count. When people talk, they interrupt, they hesitate, they speak in monosyllables, they use grunts, ohs, ahs, sighs, and pauses. Make your dialogue sound realistic by raising your awareness of how people really speak.

Discover how the characters would speak by drawing upon your personal experiences. Think of a particular person or people from your past who remind you of your character. Recall the intonations, inflections, and rhythms of their speech, and put them into your character's dialogue.

What adjective or adverb would best describe your character? When you write dialogue, think of her speaking in terms of the adjective. If the adjective you chose was *arrogant,* then make the dialogue alive with arrogant phrases and rejoinders. If the adjective you chose was *charming,* then make your character's dialogue sound friendly, smooth, and slick.

Finding the right adjective will help you discover the dominant attitude of the character, which will be expressed through the dialogue. Concentrate on mannerisms, behaviors, gestures, and the way he communicates. Is his voice gruff? Does he speak quickly, avoiding eye contact? Does he talk in a loud voice or a whisper?

By answering these questions, you'll begin to create dialogue that is original. You'll give each character his or her own voice, which will have the ring of truth.

Five Tips for Writing Good Dialogue

1. Dialogue must be dramatic.

2. Dialogue is best when it creates arguments, fights, and explosions of emotion between your characters.

3. Have conflict and tension in your dialogue.

4. Use incomplete sentences.

5. Use slang and colloquialism.

In scripts, plays, and teleplays, dialogue is spoken. Listen to it when you go to films and plays. Start to discover why some dialogue sounds good and some doesn't work. In plays, the writer uses more metaphors, similes, and imagery in the dialogue. Dialogue carries the conflict in a play. Vary the dialogue. Make it lyrical; make it mundane. Give your dialogue a beat, rhythm, pulse, intonation, inflection, cadence. At times, dialogue should sing; at other times, it should zing.

Voice

When I refer to the voice of each character, I'm referring to the truth of that character. What is he expressing about himself, and what is his point of view?

The voices of your characters allow you to express your own truth, passion, and vision through them. Get in touch with all the different voices residing inside you and let them resound through your characters.

Subtext

Since dialogue should be emotional rather than conversational, one of the best ways of writing it is by using subtext. Subtext allows your audience to identify with your characters emotionally.

In our daily life, most of us aren't direct. We often don't say how we feel because we're afraid we'll hurt the other person. Subtext is the unspoken feelings beneath the spoken words.

Writing with subtext is the best type of writing, because so much is happening beneath the dialogue. It gives room for others to bring to the story their own emotions and feelings about what is being said or done. Haven't we all felt the pain of being rejected? Haven't we all felt the uneasiness of trying to end a relationship and not knowing how? Of course we have! In fact, in most of our daily contacts, we use subtext, especially when emotions and feelings are involved.

Subtext is also used in actions. When your character doesn't say what she feels, she might go to her desk and start slamming things around or furiously sharpen pencils. There is subtext in her actions!

Every good film or book is loaded with subtext. It is subtle, and is not sarcasm or being snide. When you use subtext, the audience knows there is more going on in a scene than what is said. Subtext is the *emotional undertone* beneath the words when the characters are behaving differently from the way they're feeling. The subtext is the emotional undercurrent, such as rage, joy, sorrow, or fear, beneath the character's actions and words. By learning to write subtext, you'll have the best type of dialogue possible.

Writing Takes Practice

> "Habit is habit, and not to be flung out the window . . . but coaxed downstairs a step at a time."
>
> —Mark Twain

Writing is a habit, and it takes practice to improve. By learning the craft, you will have a blueprint or guide to follow, so you can transform your ideas into an exciting story. You will soon be able to develop characters with a goal, who are in conflict with one another and ultimately reach a resolution—hopefully, a successful one.

If you are willing to work steadily and persistently at learning the craft of writing, you will succeed as a writer.

The Emotional Line

In every good story, there is an emotional connection between the main character and another major character. Even in action-adventure films, when there is strong action *plus* a powerful emotional relationship between the main character and another character, you have greater depth, you have fireworks, you have drama! A good story includes both plot and an emotional aspect of that makes us care about the characters.

We hope the hero and heroine will overcome the danger together, but by the end of their journey, we are also rooting for these two characters to get together in a relationship.

CHAPTER FIVE

Everything You Wanted to Know About Characters: From Heroes to Villains

"I always begin with a character, or characters, and then try to think up as much action for them as possible."

—John Irving

Creating characters is an exciting and challenging writing goal. I believe that it's the characters who make a story successful. You certainly remember the characters of a film, play, or book long after you have forgotten the plot.

Just like human beings, the characters you create need to be multifaceted. You must add layers to your characters as you write them. Give each character a many-sided personality, with contradictions and complexities. Keep reading to learn how to create incredible characters.

The Protagonist and the Antagonist

All good stories have a protagonist (hero) and an antagonist (villain). An exciting story consists of conflict between the main character and another character. Even children's books have a protagonist and an antagonist, such as Goldilocks and the three bears or Little Red Riding Hood and the big, bad wolf.

Whether you're writing books, movie scripts, or plays, you should always include a protagonist and an antagonist. Westerns usually have the conflict between the cowboys and the Indians or the railroad and the cattlemen. In murder mysteries, it's usually between the private eye and the criminal. In horror stories, the conflict is between the mad scientist, mummy, or monster and the hero. Audiences love this type of conflict because it gives them someone to root for and someone to fear.

In every well-written story, the protagonist has a desperate goal to reach and the antagonist stands in his way. You must develop clear contrasts between your protagonist and antagonist. If you have someone to love, you need someone to hate, and each character must be of equal strength for you to have exciting, emotional conflict. The stakes between your protagonist and your antagonist must be high or your conflict will be weak.

Your characters should be well-balanced—your villain can't be all bad, and your hero can't be all good. Make sure your hero has vulnerabilities and weaknesses. He must have a flaw or two so he'll be interesting. Perhaps he could possess a character trait he needs to overcome to reach his goal. Or make him human by giving him a bad temper or having him be insecure even though he's a general in the United States Army. Likewise, your antagonist needs to have some good qualities. He can't be all bad.

The Main Character

After teaching thousands of students, I want to stress the importance of having only one main character or protagonist in your story. Why? Because you are telling a story through the main character. And although you will have other characters in your story, it still is one character's journey. How do you know who your main character is? Answer the following questions:

1. Does my main character have a specific goal that she or he desperately wants to achieve?

2. Is my main character active, not reactive, throughout the story?

3. Does my main character change or have a transformation in the climax?

If you've answered yes, to all the questions, you've chosen the right main character. By answering these questions, you'll find a purpose for your character.

Now that you've determined who your main character is, you'll want to find the best adjective to describe your hero's dominant personality trait. Find a thesaurus and make a list of all the adjectives that are appropriate for your character's personality. Study them and then choose the adjective that describes your character's dominant personality trait. Every time your character is in a particular situation in your story, think of the adjective that you've chosen, so you can get a better handle on how your character will behave. You will see how consistent and realistic your characters will become in all situations and conflicts.

The Character's Goal

The main character's goal will drive the story forward. The goal provides the motivation that enables the character to change in the climax. A story would certainly be boring if the main character did nothing but remain passive and reactive. To make your main character active, this goal has to be one that she desperately wants to reach in the climax.

The goal determines the action and creates the story. For example, in a mystery, a crime is committed, and the main character, the detective, wants to solve the crime. In the end, the story is resolved when the detective discovers the guilty person.

You can see how the goal is the catalyst that gives your main character the thrust and momentum to drive the story and keep your readers or viewers interested.

The goal gives your story action, energy, and a destination. The goal you choose for your main character is really the plot structure for the story. Does the character want to be a movie star, to overcome fear of water, or to have a boyfriend? Choosing the right goal for your characters will give you the ability to tell a great story.

Your main character's goal must be specific. To say that your character's goal is love, power, or money is too abstract and vague. If your character wants love, it must be the love of a certain person, just as Romeo desperately wants the love of Juliet.

Power is another goal that is too broad and abstract. But if you say to yourself, "My main character wants to become a composer like the teacher in *Mr. Holland's Opus,* or "She wants the love of the president of the United States, as in *The American President,* you're now being specific. The goal sets off your story from the beginning to the end! The stronger the goal, the higher the stakes, the more conflict and tension your characters will experience and the more involved your readers and viewers will be.

Character Motivation

Writers often don't know how to motivate their characters' behavior. This leads to inconsistent and unbelievable characters. Your character's actions must be consistent with his or her personality. To achieve this consistency, you must ask such questions as, Why would my character behave this way? What would motivate my character to do such and such? What makes my character a criminal?

As the writer, you must find the right answers. If you don't know why your characters behave as they do, you won't ever make them real or believable. Too many writers just start writing without even thinking about the character's motivation, and they usually create stereotypical characters who don't work. It's amazing what human beings are capable of doing under the right circumstances, especially in life-and-death situations. Given the proper motivation and the right circumstances, your characters could do anything. Develop a history for them to help you understand their drives, desires, and fears.

The Back Story

Characters come to your story with a past, a childhood, a family, and life experiences. As a writer, you must know all about each character's background to understand what motivates him in the present. So before you write your story, take time to plan out the motivation and the hidden intentions of all your characters.

Just as a psychologist asks questions to get a patient's case history, you must ask questions of each of your characters to get his or her past history. Who raised him? Did she have a happy childhood? Where did she grow up? Were his parents divorced or happily married? Did he have any brothers or sisters, or was he the only child?

Start looking for cause-and-effect connections between your character's inner life and outer world. Is your character playing a role, or is he being authentic? How your character deals with his internal and external world will depend upon his ability to handle frustration and overcome obstacles.

What do you know about your characters' lives *before* you open your story? What did they do? How did they earn a living? Where do your characters come from? Is their back story interesting? Will it be revealed in your plot?

After you have developed a character's history and completed his biography, you will want to study the relationship between the character's external self and internal self.

The Psychology of Characters

There is more to writing a story than creating a plot and characters. As a writer, you need to understand psychology so you'll be on the road to creating compelling, complex, and credible characters. Think not only about your characters' social and physical aspects but also about their internal life. Ask yourself if a particular character is an extrovert or an introvert. Do you have a handsome ladies' man who feels ugly inside? Is your kindly grandfather ready to explode?

Are your characters self-doubting, narcissistic, secure, fearful, angry, loving, bitter, or depressed? You need to develop their psychology to avoid stock characters. Give them internal problems, so they become complex and realistic. Are they egotistical or shy? Do they behave in a selfish manner, or are they people pleasers?

As a writer, you are always probing more deeply inside your character's skin, always questioning her behavior, behaving like a psychologist. You are searching for reasons for her actions and creating motivation for them. After you have developed the past history for your character and completed her biography, you will want to study the relationship between her external self and internal self.

Observe people around you, at work, home, and play, and use the knowledge you gain to put yourself inside your character's head and get to understand what she thinks and feels. Peel away the protection layers as you put your character under pressure. Strip your character of her defenses and watch what she does.

With today's worldly and sophisticated audiences, you must have knowledge of such psychological issues as death, divorce, rape, incest, alcoholism, abuse, and dysfunctional relationships. These and other mental-health issues are frequently written about in today's scripts, especially the real-life stories on television. As a writer, you must understand the psychological effects of such issues. All of these issues must be dealt with honestly and openly, so they'll be believable and emotionally truthful.

The Character Biography

Before you begin your story, you must develop extensive biographies for all of your major characters. This will enable you to discover what past experiences they have had and how those experiences affect them now. Ask questions about whether they were popular in school, whether they had a good home life, whether they were good in sports. These are just a few examples of how to investigate your characters' past. Knowing the answers to these questions will give your characters a back story for you to draw from.

The three categories for the character biography are the physical, the social, and the emotional. As you develop each category, you'll get to know your characters.

The Physical

The physical aspects of a character are rather basic. They include height, weight, hair color, eye color, manner of walking, talking, eating, smiling, body language, mannerisms, gestures, posture. What is his overall appearance? Is he handsome, ugly, pretty, weak, strong, stocky, fat, thin?

Before you attribute particular physical traits to a character, delve into his personality. His appearance affects the way he feels about himself and how he behaves in society. Think about the physical types of characters you need for your story and then develop realistic, consistent physical traits that make their behavior authentic.

The Social

The social aspects of your characters include economics, religion, race, politics, family, environment, avocation, and vocation. They include all of a character's outside interests, as well as his status in the world

What does he do with his leisure time? How does he spend his vacations? Is he upper-class or lower-class? Is he an intellectual or illiterate?

The importance of knowing your character's social standing is obvious. How characters see themselves and how others view them are based in large part on their social and economic position.

The Emotional

Discovering the emotional life of your character means knowing the person behind the mask. And isn't that what writing is all about, peeling away the layers to reveal the real person underneath?

The emotional life of your characters will determine how they'll act and react during stressful situations. An insecure person will behave in a different manner from a confident person in the same situation. Until you can understand the emotional makeup of your characters, you won't be able to develop the right internal motivation for their behavior.

The emotional aspects of a character include his feelings of self-worth. Is he confident or insecure? Extroverted or introverted? Does he act foolish, boisterous, or fearful? Successful writing is based on powerful emotional relationships and behavior. Understand the importance of comprehending your character's emotional world.

The Emotional Pole-to-Pole Development

A character's emotional pole-to-pole development is his progression from one emotion in the opening of the story to a different emotion in the end. Many people also refer to this as the character's "arc." For example, a character might go from indifferent or selfish to caring and loving, from revenge to love, or from fear to courage.

Always give your main character a particular emotion in the opening of your story. If you choose fear or insecurity, your character should experience courage or security by the end. This kind of emotional transformation allows your reader or viewer to feel satisfied, while giving your story depth.

In the next chapter, we are going to discuss fiction techniques and all the various story forms for those of you who want to become fiction writers.

CHAPTER SIX

Fiction: From Short Stories to Poetry

"Fiction reveals truths that reality obscures."

—*Jessamyn West*

Short stories, novellas, essays, articles, and all other types of writing must have a beginning, a middle, and an end. This is the structure of every genre. Fiction writers must be able to write a good story, because without a story, there is nothing. Unfortunately, many fiction writers begin their work without having any idea where they are going. Perhaps they know only the opening sentence or have just a vague idea of what they want to write. They usually won't succeed, because laying out the story is the most difficult part of writing. Let's see how you write fiction.

Short Stories

If you want to try your hand at writing fiction, a good place to begin is with a short story. A short story is a short narrative prose and can range from a short short to a longer one. Short stories are limited in time, situation, and number of characters. You could write a character study or a story about a single event or a moment in time. But whatever you write, you must tell a story and emotionally involve your reader. Just because it's short does not make it easy. In fact, writing a complete short story with a beginning, a middle, and an end is very difficult to do in a limited amount of space and time.

The need to hook your readers immediately is a real challenge. You must be sure that what you're writing has conflict, that your characters are interesting, and that your story is about something specific.

Ask yourself, "What is this short story about?" Are you able to express the answer in a couple of sentences? If not, you shouldn't begin until you have a focus. Many people begin to write without an end in mind, and their story is all over the place.

When you write a short story, you don't have the luxury of meandering about until you discover the gist of it. You must start your problem or conflict immediately. The closer you start your story to the end, the more excitement and conflict you'll create.

A good way to familiarize yourself with this type of writing is to read short-story anthologies and study the techniques and style of the various writers. Some writers famous for their short stories are O. Henry, Sherwood Anderson, Ernest Hemingway, Flannery O'Connor, Ring Lardner, William Faulkner, Dorothy Parker, and Henry James.

Some excellent short stories are "The Lottery," by Shirley Jackson; "The Haircut," by Ring Lardner; "The Killers," by Ernest Hemingway; and "The Bear," by William Faulkner.

You usually don't have to query editors or publishers for short stories but can send them your completed manuscript, accompanied by a short cover letter.

Unfortunately, short stories are difficult to sell, since the market for them isn't as big as it was years ago. Most major magazines, such as *Esquire, The New Yorker,* and *Cosmopolitan,* don't take unsolicited manuscripts; instead, they assign stories to well-known authors. If you want to write for these magazines, you'll need to have your stories or articles submitted through an agent.

However, there are many small presses and magazines that will buy your stories without an agent. A list of small presses is given in another chapter.

A good resource for learning about the market for short-story submissions is *Novel and Short Story Writer's Market,* published by Writer's Digest Books.

Novels

If you want to try a longer form, a novella or novel is the way to go. When writing a novel, you are dealing with many more characters and many subplots. Writing a novel is like juggling. The trick is to keep all the balls in the air at the same time.

When writing a novel, you may have as many pages as you want to complete your work. You may have as few as a hundred pages or as many as a thousand. You can begin with one character's story and change to another's on the same page. You can go back and forth in time, from present to past to future, in the same chapter. You can devote pages just to describing the scenery, the setting, or the characters. You can take chapters to reveal your characters' inner thoughts and feelings, writing in a stream-of-consciousness style and playing God.

When writing a novel, you may go in any direction you choose, taking side trips along the way and zigzagging back and forth from beginning to end. A novel will be read by someone who can put the book down for an hour, a day, or a week and pick it up again at any time, so it doesn't matter how long it takes to read the book.

As a fiction writer, you're writing for the "I want it now" generation—people who don't want to spend a lot of time on extraneous details. They're used to television, McDonalds, and ATM machines and not used to waiting. Most novels written today are not filled with descriptions that go on for page after page, as novels once were.

Today's readers like the stage to be set and to see the action unfold in the present, as if viewing a scene on television and in a movie. They don't want the author to tell them what's happening; they want to see the characters play out the scene before their eyes.

There is no one way to approach writing a novel. Some people outline their novel before writing a single sentence. Others have a vague idea of what they want to write about and just start writing. Some writers do extensive research before they start their novels, and others work on their individual characters and their biographies, conflicts, and goals, while saving their research for later. In any case, what you must know before writing any story is how you want it to end. Does the criminal get caught? Does the boy get the girl?

The novel must have cause-and-effect writing, too. The biggest problem I've seen with both beginners and professional writers is that their writing is episodic. There's no spine that holds the writing together.

When writing a novel, your main character must always have a goal he or she desperately wants to reach. By giving the main character a goal, you will hold your reader's interest until the end of your book.

In a novel, you may have many subplots going on at the same time, and they, too, should be tied to the main story line. "Show it, don't tell it" is the caveat for the modern fiction writer.

The Chapter Outline

All the chapters in a book build upon one another. However, unlike scenes in a script, the chapters don't have to go in a direct line. You can meander about, going on side trips with the subplots along the way.

Each chapter must have a beginning, a middle, and an end leading to the next chapter. At the end of each chapter, the reader should want to turn the page to find out what comes next. Although each chapter in a fiction or nonfiction book should stand alone, it must also evolve from the preceding chapters.

The novelist can develop a chapter outline and write a few sentences to highlight the essence of the chapter. This outline starts at chapter one and continues to the end of the book, creating a blueprint for your novel.

Some writers use a large bulletin board to set up their chapter outline, and others use the floor. Other writers prefer three-by-five-inch note cards.

I constantly urge the writers I coach to create an outline before beginning their manuscript or script. You should, too. An outline will save you from getting blocked or taking the wrong turn in your novel. Your outline doesn't have to be written in stone. Make it loose enough so that you can change it along the way. An outline is like a piece of clay—it mustn't be too rigid or it will dry up. Let yours be an outline-in-progress, and allow yourself to change it when it doesn't work.

Point of View

In script writing you always tell your story through the main character's point of view. When writing a novel, you can change your point of view from one character to another, although you still need to focus on the main character's story.

With the omniscient viewpoint, the writer plays God and can be in every character's head. The author knows everything there is to know about everyone in the story. The problem with the omniscient viewpoint is that it tends to be rather impersonal, and the reader doesn't identify as closely with the characters as in other viewpoints. It also creates distance between the author and the characters, as well as the author and the readers.

Another point of view is the first person, which uses "I." One of the difficulties in using the first-person viewpoint is that he or she must be in every scene, and the author can never be in another person's head. The character who tells the story doesn't have the freedom to write about situations unless he or she is experiencing them.

The first-person point of view is often used for the personal story or memoir. An advantage of this viewpoint is that it speaks directly to the reader, making the writing very personal. A disadvantage is that the word *I* can get very repetitious and boring. In fact, it can be annoying if it is not cleverly used.

The most popular viewpoint is the third person, in which "he" or "she" is used. This is a personal viewpoint that is easier to handle than the first person or the omniscient point of view. The reader is easily able to identify with the characters and can feel what emotions they are experiencing.

As the author, you can't keep switching viewpoints, because it gets confusing. When writing a novel, you can change your point of view from one character to another, but you still need to focus on the main character's story. Even when using the third-person point of view, the story should be about one main character. And in the scenes with the main character, you should stress his or her viewpoint.

When you finish writing a scene about a particular character, you can skip a line to indicate the start of a new scene written from another character's point of view.

Novels Into Film

Today, with the popularity of novels being made into films, many novelists might adapt their own works if only they knew how. If a novelist thinks visually and writes chapters as a scriptwriter writes scenes, putting the action on stage, he will have a greater chance of adapting his novel to the screen.

During the past decade, it has become increasingly common to turn books into films and films into books. In either case, the adaption has to deal with structure. A good source from which to learn about adapting novels into scripts is Linda Seger's book *The Art of Adaptation.*

Mainstream Fiction

Contemporary mainstream novels, with their conventional stories, numerous subplots, and large casts of characters, are referred to as the big books. They include the popular fiction of Judith Krantz, Danielle Steele, Jackie Collins, and Sandra Brown.

Category Fiction

Novels that fit into a specific genre, such as romance, science fiction, western, mystery, thriller, gothic, historical, and so on, are referred to as category fiction.

The Mystery Novel

In a detective story, a crime is usually committed and must be solved. That is the basis for suspense and mystery.

Let's look at an example. If in the opening of the script a murder has taken place, the goal of the detective, Mr. Private Eye, is to find out who committed the murder. This sets off the story and provides the plot structure. It is the driving force and gives our main character his action. But if solving a crime is all the story is about, it will have little depth. There are many mysteries that are just like this. The only goal is for the detective to solve the crime. These types of stories have been done thousands of times. They offer nothing fresh and original.

On the other hand, if in the process of solving the crime the detective learns something important about himself and experiences an emotional change, you have a much deeper story, one that allows your character to have more of an emotional impact on the reader, who hopefully identifies with him.

The mystery category includes suspense and horror stories and psychological thrillers. The following is an organization for mystery writers:

Mystery Writers of America
17 East 47th Street, Sixth Floor
New York, New York 10017
(212) 888-8171

Active members include published fiction or nonfiction writers in the mystery genre. There are also affiliate members who haven't been published but who are mystery or crime writers.

Romance Novels

While doing research on the Internet, I accidentally came upon an area devoted to romance writers. There were guidelines from every major publisher in the field, as well as a wealth of information about how to submit your work.

There are many subcategories within the broad category of the romance novel. Each subcategory has its own rules and guidelines for the story, the romance, the sexual relationships, and the setting. It's important for you to learn the rules for each category, so that you won't waste the publisher's and your own time by sending the wrong type of romance to the wrong publisher. Some of the large publishers of romance fiction are Avon, Harlequin, Ballantine, Silhouette, and Avalon. You can write each publisher for the rules of the subcategory you're interested in, or you can get guidelines and instructions for submitting your manuscript from the romance writers site on America Online. This field is vast and still growing. It accounts for a major part of women's book purchases.

The field of romance gives new writers wonderful opportunities to get published. In addition, there are support systems and networking groups for romance writers, including the regional and local chapters of the Romance Writers of America.

A few years ago, I was asked to speak at a gathering of the Romance Writers of Orange County in California. I thought about fifty people might show up, and to my surprise, there were well over three times that number. The room was crowded with enthusiastic romance writers. I had planned my speech about the fundamentals of writing and was scheduled to speak after the business meeting. The second surprise I had was when the chairperson asked for those who had recently been published to stand. It seemed as if half the participants stood up. I quickly had to change my topic so as not to insult them!

The following is a national organization for romance writers:

Romance Writers of America
137000 Veterans Memorial Drive, No. 315
Houston, Texas 77014

Children's Writing

Children's literature is a highly specialized field. In general, publishers ask for writing that is age appropriate, unforced, concrete, and original. Publishers often get children's writing that is hackneyed, trite, and second-rate. Perhaps inexperienced writers don't think you need to adhere to the same standards when writing for children as you do for adults. Wrong. You need good, clear, concrete, original writing for children, just as you do for adults. I've consulted with many writers of children's books, ranging from picture books to young-adult novels. The most important advice I can give to those of you who want to compete in this market is not to take any shortcuts. Respect your readers, and be able to identify what would interest children at the age level you're writing for. Don't lump children's writing all together. There are picture books, books for preschoolers, books for middle-school children, and young-adult novels.

For younger children, you need to use specifics and not deal with abstract ideas. Your language must be colorful, rhythmic, and clear. Your characters should be well-defined, not ambiguous. Appeal to the five senses of your young readers and they will respond to your writing.

In the Cinderella story, you know how badly the wicked stepmother behaves toward Cinderella and how differently she treats her own daughters. It is clear that the fairy godmother is Cinderella's friend and that the prince loves her. Nothing is ambiguous. Nothing is abstract. The story is told through characters that are consistent and precise.

The most important quality of writing for children is that it touches your readers and lets them identify with "the little engine that could," or Bambi or the heroine of *Beauty and the Beast*.

Whether you're writing about the Tin Man, the Cowardly Lion, Hansel and Gretel, or the "wild things," your characters must be realistic, and their story must have emotional conflict. You want to connect with your readers' emotions and have them identify with your characters, whether they are animals, boats, or genies.

Younger children like to hear words that create a rhythm or a beat. Words that have movement and meter are great to write. Do you remember how, when you were a young child, you and other children would talk in singsong? For example, in the story "The Three Little Pigs," the big bad wolf says, "Little pig, little pig, let me come in." And the little pig responds, "Not by the hair of my chinney chin chin." Such sayings become an integral part of a story, and are also important because of the rhythm and rhyme.

Whether you want to write for preschoolers or school-age children, the best way to break into the children's market is to go to the local library and study the books targeted to the population for whom you want to write.

Young-Adult Novels

Writing for the young-adult market takes just as much craft and character development as writing for the adult market. Judy Blume, a well-known writer for young adults, is a wonderful example of someone who *doesn't* write down to children. She writes for the young adult reader with respect. She also has a pulse on the subjects her readers want to read about and has the ability to know exactly what emotional situations and relationships they are experiencing. Her fictional characters are realistic, and their issues attract young adults who are experiencing similar situations.

As a writer of novels for young adults, you must empathize with what they are experiencing in their lives. Above all, don't patronize or write down to younger readers. Put yourself in their shoes, and recall how you felt at a particular age.

A young-adult novel usually runs from 150 to 250 pages. The story should have well-drawn characters, with goals, conflicts, obstacles, and a resolution.

Surprisingly, in spite of the omnipresent television set, many children are reading and want to be read to. Here are some publishers who specialize in children's literature and magazines:

Cricket
P.O. Box 300
Peru, Illinois 61354

This magazine, founded in 1973, includes stories, articles, illustrations, and poetry for ages nine through twelve.

Farrar, Straus & Giroux
Books For Young Readers
19 Union Square West
New York, New York 10003

This publisher was established in 1946 and occasionally produces book-length children's poetry.

Highlights for Children
803 Church Street
Honesdale, Pennsylvania 18431

This venerable monthly magazine features stories, articles, and short poems for ages two through twelve.

Society of Children's Book Writers and Illustrators
345 North Maple Drive, Suite 296
Beverly Hills, CA 90210
(310) 859-9887

Science Fiction and Fantasy

Just because you're writing science fiction or fantasy doesn't mean you don't have to create a good story. Even though your characters may be aliens from outer space or monsters from the lower depths, you still must know the craft of storytelling.

I've worked with many writers who seem to think that if they're writing in this genre they can make fantastic events happen without motivating the characters or telling an emotional story. Remember that a good story allows the reader to identify with its characters.

Whatever world you present to your readers or viewers, whether it's another planet peopled with aliens or a world filled with man-eating plants, you must have a well-crafted story with a beginning, a middle, and an end. And the characters must move your story toward a satisfying conclusion.

Don't take shortcuts by using magic tricks or weird characters to do the work you must do. You need to maintain all the high standards you would use for any other type of writing, using complex characters and telling a well-plotted story. You can make your reader believe in anything if your writing is clear and your characters involving.

You usually don't need an agent to submit short science-fiction stories. A few magazines will publish stories from new writers. They include *Amazing Stories Magazine, Omni, Analog,* and *Isaac Asimov's Science Fiction* magazine.

There is also a national organization for science fiction writers. It is:

Science Fiction Writers of America
P.O. Box 4236
West Columbia, South Carolina 29171

Poetry

"The poet is the rock of defense for human nature."

—*William Wordsworth*

If you want to become a published poet, there are many opportunities. Chapbooks are a popular way for poets to self-publish. They can range from typewritten pages stapled together to extravagant books, illustrated and professionally bound.

Today, poetry is usually written in blank verse or free verse. It differs from prose in the way it's laid out on the page.

Many people make the mistake of thinking that since much poetry doesn't rhyme, all you have to do to write a poem is to set it down on the page in stanza form. Well, this isn't the case. Poetry needs to have meter, imagery, and rhythm.

Poetry is powerful and passionate. It resonates with you while you read it. Poetry depends upon the right word to make it work. Poetry creates sound patterns and rhythms. It is meant to be read silently or aloud, using language that is lyrical and metrical, like a song. A group of syllables constitute a foot of poetry. The number of feet determines the measure of a line.

The first thing I ever published was a poem I wrote in a poetry workshop. Looking back, I realize that it was published because it emotionally touched the readers.

People write poetry for many reasons. Some write to inform, others to teach a moral, to share a philosophy of life, to entertain, to experience a catharsis, or to demonstrate the human condition. Some poems tell a story; some describe a person, place, or thing. Poetry concerns feelings—love, hate, lust, greed, sorrow, joy, loneliness, despair. Poetry is about spirit, nature, imagination, creativity, life, and death.

The power of the poem resonates in a person's soul. When I was conducting poetry workshops for the elderly, I saw proof that poetry was often more powerful than therapy. Many people who wouldn't ordinarily share their feelings did so through the poetry. Just writing down their feelings and emotions allowed them to honor what they felt. The poetry was a vehicle for their suppressed emotions.

Follow common-sense rules when you submit your poems. For instance, be neat, and include a self-addressed, stamped envelope, a cover letter, and three to five poems per submission. Put only one poem on a page.

To find publishers who are currently accepting poetry, consult *Poet's Market* (Writer's Digest Books) or *The Directory of Poetry*

Publishers (Dustbooks). Both directories are published annually and should be available at your local library. Two other helpful publications are *Poet's & Writer's Magazine* and *American Poets and Fiction Writers*. Both are published by:

Poets and Writer's Inc.
72 Spring Street, Room 301
New York, New York 10012
(212) 226-3586

One of the oldest magazines around is *Poetry,* founded in 1912. The editors allow submissions of up to four poems. The address is:

Poetry
60 West Walton Street
Chicago, Illinois 60610

A national organization for poets is:

Academy of American Poets
584 Broadway, Suite 1208
New York, New York 10012
(212) 274-0343

Cards

"Poets were the first teachers of mankind."

—Horace

Greeting cards often have rhymes in the message, but often aren't considered poetry. A rhyme consists of using a pair of words which end with the same sound. For example, day, play, say, may, gay, ray, all start with a different letter, but end with the same sound.

Usually the verse or saying conveys a single thought, which is expressed to the reader. If you want to write for greeting-card companies, you need to be able to express a thought or feeling in a few words. Always keep the reader in mind and ask yourself, "What is the purpose of this card?" Is it to express a feeling of joy, sadness, loneliness, friendship, hope, love? Or is the card for a specific occasion, such as a birthday, an anniversary, Valentine's Day, or Mother's Day? Is your message clear and fresh? Do you say something old in a new way?

A Guide to Greeting Card Writing, edited by Larry Sandman for Writer's Digest Books, offers a checklist of what to watch out for when you write verses or notes for cards.

CHAPTER SEVEN

Nonfiction: From Self-Help to How-Tos

"Good writing is true writing."

—*Ernest Hemingway*

What better way to reach millions of people and develop professional recognition than by writing an article, a professional paper, or a book? But before you do, you should do your homework and find out what's already on the market. Then you must learn to write what editors, publishers, and the general public want to read.

Free-lancing

Free-lancing is a business like any other. Whether you want to be a free-lance writer of magazine or newspaper articles, it's a competitive field and takes courage to succeed.

When submitting a manuscript for publication, be certain it is professionally formatted and written in the best possible way. Since you have so little control over the process, you must at least be able to submit a top-rated product.

There's no point in free-lancing if you aren't a self-starter. Since you aren't facing outside pressure or deadlines, there is nobody standing over your shoulder giving you pep talks. It all has to start with you. Your desire to be published must be strong enough to carry you through the obstacles you will face in the world of free-lance writing.

If you're writing an article, the first thing to do is to find out whether your subject is current. If you're writing about the me generation in the 1990s, when spirituality is the trend, you probably will not sell your piece. On the other hand, if you're on the cutting edge of a trend, chances are you will sell your work, assuming it's well-crafted.

Timing is all-important. I recall a situation in which an editor loved my nonfiction book and wanted to make a deal, but the subject matter didn't happen to fit into the publisher's marketing plan for that quarter, and so my book wasn't purchased.

This is written not to discourage you but to encourage you to do whatever it takes to become a successful free-lancer. To be a free-lance writer requires initiative and perseverance. You must create an action plan to sell your work. Just like any other business where you work for yourself, you must develop a marketing strategy for your product.

If you have an article idea or subject that fits the editor's needs and you're able to identify a trend as it's emerging, your writing will have a good chance of being published.

Ask yourself if your topic is of interest to the general population. Does what you have written fit into the marketing plan of the publisher? Do the editors have a slot in their catalog for a book like yours? If you are fortunate, your book will fill the need of a publishing house.

Since publishers are in the business of selling books and magazines, you have to make your product easy for them to buy. They must feel that your product can be profitable. The bottom line is the bottom line in the writing business.

After you decide what topic you are going to write about, you need to discern which magazine might want to publish your article. Part of being a successful free-lancer is to know your market and target your writing for it. You wouldn't dream of writing an article on how to meet a man for *Family Circle*, nor would you send an article on knitting to *Sports Illustrated*.

Study the different magazines and find a couple that seem just right for your topic. Then go to the library and read back issues of the magazine until you familiarize yourself with its writing style, slant, and point of view. What type of readership does it have? What age group does it target? Is it geared toward men, women, or children? If the magazine is a literary one, you wouldn't use slang and humor.

You also have to become an expert on the subject you're writing about. Read other articles on the same topic, and study the market so you will have a fresh slant.

Personally, I believe you should submit your proposal or article to a number of magazines, so that you won't waste months waiting for a response. The worst that could happen is that everybody you submitted to would want to buy your piece and you'd have to make the choice (in your dreams!). Otherwise, it could take a year for three or even fewer companies to get back to you, and by then your article could be passé.

So if you want to break into free-lance writing, I suggest you start with writing articles. These articles can often lead to much bigger projects. An article in *Esquire* magazine in the 1970s about disco dancing became the basis for the hit movie *Saturday Night Fever*. Articles can and do lead to book deals and television series.

Before I wrote my book *Blueprint for Writing*, I had been a columnist for the *Hollywood Scriptwriter*, an international newsletter for screenwriters. My columns eventually became the material for chapters of the book.

If you are knowledgeable about a particular subject, such as cooking, marketing, therapy, letter writing, computers, quilting, communication, or dreams, create a "how to" article about it. As an expert, you could sell your article, if it is well written and interesting to the readership. Both daily and weekly newspapers are always interested in such articles.

Get ideas for articles by paying attention to the present trends in your life and how they reflect what's happening in the population in general. Ask yourself, "What's going on in my life, or with my friends, that would be of interest to others?" The 1980s were definded by the me generation; in the 1990s, the emphasis is on low-fat eating, personal responsibility, safe sex, dating in the age of AIDS, and family values.

Magazine Writing

"There are no dull subjects. There are only dull writers."

—*H.L. Mencken*

There are two kinds of magazines to write for:

1. Large, mainstream ones like *Self, New Woman, Esquire, Harper's Bazaar,* and *Vanity Fair.*

2. Smaller magazines like Sunday magazines in newspapers, or trade magazines.

It's probably easier to break into free-lance writing by targeting the special-interest magazine rather than the general-interest market. Anything you specialize in or any hobby you have could make an interesting how-to article. At present, multimedia and interactive computers are hot topics. If you are an expert in one of these fields you could write articles about the Internet explosion.

When writing articles, it helps to interview individuals for their personal stories and experiences. Be certain that you research and learn what books and articles are already out on the subject about which you're writing. Try to bring a new and fresh perspective.

Always have a positive side to your article after you've presented the problems. Your article needs to have a positive resolution, and hopefully your readers will learn something new.

When you start to write, you need a couple of paragraphs that sum up your article. You may begin with yourself and your ideas, but hopefully you'll be writing about a universal subject. Your goal is to find the unique in the universal.

1. The first paragraph of an article is personal.

2. The second paragraph is general. Everyone will relate to it. This creates commonality between you and the reader.

Reading is a wonderful way to get article ideas. If you want to write for a particular magazine, read every issue you can find to be sure your article isn't duplicating one that has already been written. Be aware of the cultural climate and the fads, trends, and upcoming hot topics. Who would have thought years ago that coffee and coffeehouses would be the rage?

Feature Articles

The feature article is more personal and colorful than a straight news article. It's usually written from the writer's point of view and can be slanted to what the writer believes. Although it's based on fact and not fiction, it can be more humorous and emotional than regular news reporting.

Nonfiction Books

> "It is in men as in soil, where sometimes there is a vein of gold, which the owner know not of."
>
> —*Jonathan Swift*

I often work with lawyers and psychotherapists to help them make their complicated or esoteric theories accessible to the general public. Too often, people are taught how to write academic papers that are dry and boring. I have spent hours teaching professionals to let go of that dry style and put their concepts, ideas, and professional experiences into dramatic and exciting nonfiction books.

Look at the powerful impact that writing popular nonfiction books has had on the general population and how such books have created media celebrities of their authors. The book *Men Are From Mars, Women Are From Venus,* by John Gray, has created a new way of dealing with the opposite sex. *Spontaneous Healing,* by Andrew Weil, M.D., has given us a new way of looking at illness. And *The Road Less Traveled,* by Scott Peck, has been on the bestseller list for years.

Writing nonfiction isn't just a matter of picking the right subject, because most subjects have been written about over and over. If you don't believe me, just go to your local bookstore and study the sections on cooking and psychology. When you write nonfiction books, you need to reinvent the wheel by giving a new perspective to an old subject.

Once you have found your focus, you must learn how to write your book. Here are two rules to remember: (1) Nonfiction must be as personal and emotional as fiction. (2) When you make a statement, besides the facts and historical material, you must also give personal examples that touch your reader emotionally.

Writing about your own or other people's experiences allows the reader to become involved. In your examples, use actual conversation, putting what a person says in quotes. For example, you could write the following:

> Mary Smith always wanted to be a dancer, but she didn't have the money. One day her teacher called her aside. "Mary, a secret fan of yours has donated ten thousand dollars so that you can go to New York and continue your studies."
>
> "I don't believe it. You're not serious," Mary cried.

This conversation brings more immediacy than just relating the story through narrative prose. Write dramatic anecdotes that allow your reader to identify with the individuals in your examples. You can accomplish this feat by keeping a single reader in mind and writing to him or her.

It's important to make your nonfiction writing visually appealing. Break up the text with subhead, bullets, graphs, and charts, and ask questions of your reader. Vary your paragraphs from short to long and from personal to informational.

Above all, make sure your information is accurate and up-to-date. You can use statistics and quotes from experts to substantiate your information. Questionnaires are useful for obtaining valuable information. When you use other people as sources, you must give them credit. The same holds true for books, newspaper articles, and magazines.

Keep your sentences short and concise, and use correct spelling, punctuation, and grammar. Study Strunk & White's *Elements of Style* or Harry Shaw's *Punctuate It Right*.

When you relate information, use humor, drama, concrete examples, active words, and colorful language.

Don't generalize. Use specific and unique examples to reach the universal. Don't lecture, but relate information in a conversational manner. Be sure your writing is clear, concise, friendly, and, most of all, accurate. Make your book reader-friendly and personal.

Travel Writing

Although travel writing sounds glamorous, like all writing, it's hard work and a very competitive field. However, there are many publications for you to send your travel article to, and this is an area where many new writers get published.

According to Writer's Digest, the travel writing business is a $3 trillion global business. It's America's third-largest retail industry and the world's biggest employer. It is no wonder there are so many aspiring travel writers.

Markets include auto clubs, state publications, specialized magazines like *Bicycling*, and consumer magazines, which have articles about what places give you the most for your money. There are also airline magazines, sports magazines, and magazines for retired people such as *Modern Maturity*.

You might break into the travel-writing business with a newspaper article. If you don't want to write for the travel section of your local paper, then go to the library and study the travel sections of state newspapers. After building up your portfolio of travel clips, you might want to send your article to a larger paper, such as the *Chicago Tribune* or the *New York Daily News*, both of which have travel sections.

Before you send your article to a magazine or newspaper, you should have the name of the current editor of the travel section.

After you have published many magazine or newspaper articles, you might want to venture into writing a travel book. Check your local library so that you don't duplicate an existing one. Develop an original slant to your book, or write it for specialized audiences, such as one with a common interest or age or income. Your library will also have information on what companies publish travel books. Here are a few:

Sierra Club Books
100 Bush Street
San Francisco, California 94104

Macmillan Travel
15 Columbus Circle
New York, New York 10023

Fodor's Travel Publications
201 East Fiftieth Street
New York, New York 10022

Photographs often increase your chances of selling a travel article, so you might include your personal photographs of the area you're writing about, or you could hire a free-lance photographer willing to work with you on spec. When you submit a photograph, it's best to include both a horizontal and a vertical shot.

When you write a travel article, you have to find a new approach to an old subject. Editors don't want to see the same old story about the same old place. Be creative and come up with new ideas for well-traveled places. One of the most popular styles is the insider's approach. For example, you might write about where to find the ten best bargains in a certain city, state, or country. Or you might specialize your article, either by subject (e.g. hiking, bicycling, fishing, boating) or by region.

Often you can use the same trip to yield several articles, each written from a different perspective. These individual articles can then be submitted to various publishers. And remember to avoid the clichéd "My Trip To . . . " style of writing. This approach is nothing more than a variation on the infamous "What I Did on My Summer Vacation" school essay and is a sign that you're an amateur. Avoid it! And as in all writing, be concise, clear, and current.

Personal Essays

When writing an essay, you usually want to inform or persuade. In either case, you've got to know your subject matter and be informed yourself. Despite what you may have learned about writing essays in high school and college, they don't have to be dry or boring.

What do you want to say in your essay? Many writers begin an essay without knowing how to asnwer that question. If you can't state the essence of your essay in a couple of sentences, keep working at it until you can.

Know your target audience. Do you want to influence the members of a political group? Are you trying to make a statement about the judicial system to lawyers? Or do you want to write about the effect HMOs are having on medical care for the elderly? Once you've figured out what point you want to make, you need to know who you are making it to.

Pepper your essay with personal stories or anecdotes, to make it interesting as well as informative. These stories can either introduce your essay or sum it up. They must illustrate a specific point you want to make.

An anecdote can inject humor into your essay or evoke an emotional response in the reader.

Become familiar with the essay style and learn what makes a good piece. Use strong verbs, fewer adjectives and adverbs, and concrete words, as well as correct punctuation, grammar, and spelling. Use quotes to help break up the text and give it immediacy. Use sensory writing—touch, taste, smell, sound, and sight—to evoke feelings from readers and enable them to identify with what you have to say. Isn't that the point of your essay? To get the reader to think about the subject you're writing about and to be influenced by your ideas?

Newspapers will often publish a personal essay in the Op-Ed section. Literary magazines also publish essays, and there are books of essays, which usually have a theme or a particular focus, such as playwrights writing about plays, or successful men writing essays regarding their success. The field is small, but it's not impossible to get published.

Interviews

Getting an in-depth interview with a high-profile celebrity often leads to getting your work published in a magazine or newspaper.

If you're fortunate enough to know a popular figure in sports, film, television, or politics, try to get his permission for an interview. Gather facts and do substantial research before the interview. Prepare your questions, and be sure they require more than a yes or no answer. Ask easy questions in the beginning and save the harder ones for later. Ask questions that encourage your subjects to talk about themselves in a personal way without being intrusive. Develop a good rapport before you ask tough questions.

Ask how much time you have at the beginning of the interview, because you don't want to waste a lot of valuable time on small talk. Create a safe atmosphere of trust and friendliness, and don't put your subject on the spot, especially if you want to keep the lines of communication open. It is better not to use a tape recorder, as many people feel uncomfortable when they are being recorded. You should know what direction you want to go in, but be flexible enough to change strategies if you find your subject opening up about some unexpected topic.

When referring to your notes, be as inconspicuous as possible. Allow the conversation to flow. When asking a question, learn how to listen to the answers and take notes without interfering with the interview process.

There are many opportunities for nonfiction writers to get published. Draw upon your own personal experiences and interests. Discover subjects to write about from looking at your drives and your passions. And keep sending out what you've written until you get published.

If your interests lie more in script writing than fiction or nonfiction, the next two chapters will give you all the information you need to become a successful scriptwriter.

CHAPTER EIGHT

Script Writing: From Screenplays to Sitcoms

"If you would be a reader, read; if a writer, write."

—*Epictetus*

Script writing is a craft unto itself, using a special format and a highly developed structure. A script is a narrative that tells a story through the use of moving pictures having forward-moving linear action. The story goes in a direct line from beginning to end.

In a script, the story is always told through the main character's point of view. You can't go into your character's head and tell what he or she thinks or feels. You can only show what he does (action) and says (dialogue). The author can't intrude his or her thoughts into the story.

The number of pages in a script indicates approximately how long it will take the audience to view the finished product. One page of script equals about one minute of viewing time. So if a script is 120 pages, the viewing time will be 120 minutes, or two hours.

When you begin to write a script, you should already know the ending and structure your scenes to get to the resolution as quickly as possible. Unlike a novel, a script cannot afford to wander about. You have a limited amount of time in which to tell your story. The time is usually between ninety minutes and two hours. You can see why it is so very important to tell your story and get to your destination (the end) as quickly as possible.

Structure

Structure starts with the main story or plot line. In a script, there are usually one or more interconnected subplots. If they are well-written, at the end of the script they will connect to the main plot. Laying out any story structure is the most difficult part of writing, and being able to connect everything to the main plot line is hard work.

Good structure means each scene should cause the scene that follows it and evolve from the scene that preceded it. Events in a script must arise through cause and effect and must not be contrived or happen by accident. You can't have the Greek chorus solving the problem. It has to be motivated by the story and the characters.

Think of all the scenes as pieces of a giant jigsaw puzzle, and try to connect all the pieces so that you can see the entire picture. When a script falls apart, it's because there's no blueprint; the scenes occur without connection or purpose.

Many people resist learning dramatic structure. They manage to find those few movies or novels that have been successful without being tightly structured. That is all well and good. But you must first learn the rules before you can break them. So if you want to become a successful scriptwriter, you must master the rules and techniques of classical structure.

The Three-Act Structure

When you begin to write your feature film or television movie, it will be much easier to approach your 120-page script if you put it into a three-act structure. This will make the material more manageable and give the writing better organization and direction.

Act 1

Act 1 is known as the act of exposition. It is approximately thirty pages in length. In the opening of act 1, you must set up the problem to be solved and introduce the major characters of your film. This problem will take the rest of the movie to solve. The audience must immediately know what your movie is about or they will lose interest.

Something must happen to start your story moving toward a destination. What event or problem starts your main character on a journey? Is it a death, divorce, losing a job, or meeting the person of his dreams? You need to know what your story is about and what the rules are for the players. By the end of act 1, your main character is taking action and moving forward. There is no turning back. He has made a decision to solve the problem and is moving ahead.

Act 2

Act 2 is known as the act of complications. It is the longest act, consisting of approximately sixty pages. In act 2, you must set up all of the obstacles that stand in the path of your main character. The more stumbling blocks, the harder your main character must struggle to reach his goal. In act 2, the conflict and tension must escalate. By the end of act 2, it looks as if all is lost for your main character. He is at his lowest and most desperate point. The audience is on the edge of their seats not knowing what will happen to him. He is forced to take some new and dramatic action. This act is usually the most difficult to write, and when writers get stuck, it's usually in the middle of the second act.

Act 3

Act 3 is known as the act of resolution. It is the shortest act in the script. It has approximately thirty pages or fewer. All that has gone on before is heading to the highest point of dramatic conflict—the climax. The climax is the end of your script. In act 3, the problem you set up in the opening must be resolved; your main character must experience a change, and your theme must be revealed.

In act 3, your main character makes a discovery about himself. He sees the light, so to speak. When he gets this new insight, your audience will feel satisfied.

All of the preceding scenes have been leading up to this climactic one. If the action escalates in the second act, by act 3 it *explodes.*

Going from Idea to Scenes

After you have determined your story line, how do you decide what scenes you need to write? Since there will be forty to sixty scenes or more, what do you do between the opening and the climax?

The first thing to do is to start thinking of all the possible scenes for your script. Let your imagination go wild. Then jot down every scene you could possibly use. Write everything that comes into your head in a couple of sentences for each potential scene. It doesn't matter if you discard most of them; it's getting them down without judgment that is important.

Think of all the things that could possibly happen to your main character in order for him to reach his goal. Think of your settings, characters, locations, atmosphere, and obstacles, and write them down as fast as you can. After you have jotted down all of the possibilities, then you can start putting the scenes in some sort of order.

The Scene

A scene is a unit of drama, and each scene is built upon the one preceding it. Every scene must be connected, from your opening scene, which sets up the problem, through to the climactic scene, which ends your script.

A scene, like a script, has a beginning, a middle, and an end. You can think of a scene as a miniscript, having all the same elements as an entire screenplay. In other words, your scene starts at one point of action and leads to another, which is the climax or end of your scene. Just as you do with an entire script, you need to know the ending of a scene before you start writing it.

Every scene must have a purpose. Without a purpose, the scene doesn't work and goes nowhere. Before you write a scene, ask yourself, "What is the purpose of this scene?"

Finding the purpose of your scene will help give it focus. Perhaps the purpose is to introduce a love interest, show a crime being committed, or plant a necessary clue for a detective to discover. Knowing your purpose keeps your writing solid and on track, and gives you a direction to follow.

Several scenes connected by a main action or purpose are known as a sequence of scenes. For instance, in a chase scene, there can be many locations but only one purpose—to catch someone.

The best place to start your scene is in the middle of the action! The middle of the action means exactly what it says. It is also important for you to know what you want to accomplish in the scene *before* you start writing. If you can't state the purpose of your scene, then eliminate it, because it probably isn't focused.

In the climax of a scene, something must happen, just as something happens in the climax of a script. The climax of your scene must be the most dramatic point and move the action along to the next scene. It should thrust your story forward, compelling the audience to ask, "What's going to happen next?"

The length of a scene varies. It may be as short as half a page or as long as five or more pages. Whatever the length, you should start in the middle of the action; have a single purpose; and make sure you have a beginning, a middle, and a climax.

The Treatment

A treatment is a step-by-step, detailed narrative account of your story written in present tense prose. It usually consists of twenty to fifty pages, typewritten, and double-spaced. The treatment is an expanded version of an outline, and it is written in exciting prose, detailing everything that happens in your script. A good, solid treatment includes all the action in a film. The only thing it doesn't include is the dialogue. (See Appendix A.)

Sometimes writers develop a treatment before they write a script. Take time to create an interesting, well-written treatment that will excite readers and hold their interest. When you write your treatment, show what's happening through the external action. Show us; don't tell! Your prose translates into film, so write visually. Picture each scene before writing it, and translate these images into descriptive words.

Often it is on the strength of your treatment that you'll sell your story. Don't let it be filled with weak verbs, adjectives, or adverbs. Keep the action moving, and don't slow it down by giving camera directions.

You want your treatment to be a good read. If an executive doesn't like your treatment, he certainly won't ask you to write the script.

Synopsis

The synopsis is usually less structured than an outline and often is written to accompany a feature-length script or television script. When the producer, director, publisher, or development executive doesn't want to read your entire script or manuscript, he might ask you to write a synopsis to accompany it. If he is interested in the synopsis, they will be more likely to read your script.

If you don't want to write an outline, write a synopsis, which is an overview of your story, in as little as a couple of pages or as many as ten. Writing a synopsis helps you get your story structure down in the proper order. (See Appendix D.)

Write your synopsis as you would write a short story, using the present tense.

It is often difficult to reduce your 120-page script or 430-page novel to a one-page synopsis, but if your work is well structured, you won't have any difficulty.

Step Outline

Scriptwriters create what is known as the step outline before they begin their script. A step outline describes what happens in each scene in a couple of sentences. It shows the order of the scenes and the action that happens in each one.

The scenes in your outline describe the essence of your material and create the shape or form of your structure. No scene should be included in your outline unless it serves the overall purpose. Laying out your scenes in this manner helps to develop a fast-moving, workable plot structure.

This outline is the most important aspect of story development for the screenwriter. I require all my students to use the step outline before they put a single word down in script format.

There are several ways to develop your outline. Some people like to use three-by-five-inch note cards or five-by-seven-inch note cards to write the one or two sentences for each scene. Using note cards gives you a lot of freedom, because you can move them around. Other scriptwriters use different-colored cards for each act, which helps them focus when they're laying out the cards.

The Hook or the Teaser

We live in an age of "I want it now," with fast-food deliveries, microwave dinners, and drive-through restaurants. Just push a button and you can buy anything you want on the Home Shopping Channel, get money from the ATM machine, and instantly interact with strangers via the Internet. So it's understandable that filmwriters have to hook the viewers in the first three minutes, so they won't leave the theater.

If your audience isn't hooked immediately, you have failed as a scriptwriter. You must give them something exciting at the beginning of your film. This exciting scene is known in the business as a hook.

Television shows often use what's known as a teaser to engage the audience right from the start. The teaser is usually an exciting scene that is taken out of context from the middle of the show. It contains conflict and suspense and is usually shown before the actual program starts. This is done so that the viewer will be teased into wanting to know what's going to happen next.

Script Format

The script format is a blueprint that shows what will be seen and heard. It includes the dialogue, descriptions of the characters and locations, and directions for the characters' actions. This format is different from any other. There are specific rules that must be learned and followed. You should never submit any script unless it is typewritten in script format. This is one rule that must never be broken. It is essential that you have the correct format or you won't even get your script read. (See Appendix E.)

Camera Angles

Your script should be a good and exciting read. Make it flow and involve the people who read it, so they won't want to put it down. One way to ensure the smooth flow of work is *not* to include camera angles and directions. You are the writer. Let the director or the cinematographer decide on the camera shots and angles he or she wants to use. If you include camera angles, it will lessen the impact of your script and distract your reader.

From Fade In to Fade Out

At the opening of your script, type the words "FADE IN:" in caps in the upper left-hand corner of the page. This means "Curtain rises." At the end of your script, type the words "FADE OUT:" in caps in the lower right-hand corner of the page. This means "Fade to black." These are the only times you ever use these terms. After writing "FADE IN:" skip two lines and write whether the shot will be an inside or an outside shot, the location being shot, and the time of day or night. This is referred to as the slugline. It's written in all caps and introduces each new scene.

Write "INT." for interior shot, "EXT." for exterior shot, the location, and the time. For example:

INT. RESTAURANT - DAY

or

EXT. STREET - NIGHT

After the slugline, double-space and begin to write the necessary description of the restaurant or the street. Only write what will appear in the shot.

Don't write a lot of description, but use an economy of words, describing just what must be seen. The description or direction is written in upper and lower case and is single-spaced. You write the action the same way, in upper and lower case and in prose, with active verbs, short and to the point.

When you introduce a character, use capital letters for the first and last name, and follow with a brief description of the character. "SALLY JOHNS, early thirties, blond hair and beautiful smile" could be enough description. Don't get too detailed with a character's description unless the details are an essential part of your story.

The dialogue is written in upper and lower case and centered directly under the character's name.

Parenthetical comments are written in lower case, enclosed in parentheses, and placed directly under the character's name, on a line that's separate from the dialogue.

In the directions, type camera shots or sound effects in all caps.

Some other directions you need to know are the following:

P.O.V. (point of view). If you want a shot to be from the perspective of a particular character, write, "SUSAN'S P.O.V." The camera sees what the character (in this case Susan) sees.

V.O. (voice-over). When you see a car traveling down the highway and hear a voice narrating, that is considered a voice-over. The term is used whenever you hear a character's voice but don't see him—when one character talks to another on the phone, for instance, and we hear the voice of the second character but don't see him.

O.S. (off screen). This term is used in the directions whenever we hear a sound coming from another room. It could be written in caps: "O.S. MUSIC FROM RADIO," for instance, or "O.S. SLAM-MING OF CAR DOOR."

B.G. (background) or details in the background. This is usually part of the description.

TRANSITIONS include CUT TO:, DISSOLVE TO:, MATCH CUT TO: These terms are justified on the right margin and are written all in caps.

CUT TO: Type in all caps, justified on the right margin at the end of a scene when you want to quickly cut to another. Use this and other transitions with discretion, because the slugline makes it obvious you are starting a new scene.

DISSOLVE TO: Type at the end of a scene when you want a slow change from one place to another.

MATCH CUT TO: Type this at the end of a scene before you cut to a different scene showing the same person or object as the first.

INSERT. When you need to insert a closeup of an object into the scene—in a mystery, for instance, to plant a clue or a red herring—this is the term you use.

Set the margins of your script at 15 and 75 for description and directions. Action scenes are long descriptions of what your characters are doing. When you're ready to have a character speak, double space and type the character's name in upper-case letters in the middle of the page. Write the dialogue directly under the name, with the margins set at 35 and 65. Any directions written in the dialogue are enclosed in parentheses and centered at 40 and 60. When you want to write more description or longer directions, double space and type from margin to margin (15 to 75).

If you are writing on a computer, there are programs that will give you the proper script format.

Exposition

In the first ten minutes of any film, you must give your audience information on what the film is about and who the main character is. This information, known as the exposition, needs to flow and not be intrusive. It is your job to keep your audience from walking out of the theater or turning off the television while getting it.

Avoid clichéd ways of giving information. Be creative when you write exposition. Let your mind flow and think of as many unique and clever ways to give information as you can without boring your audience.

How do you write exposition in a way that won't lose your audience? You write it with conflict and dramatic action, so your audience isn't aware you're giving them a lot of information. Instead of having your characters just discuss a problem, have them argue while speeding in a car or talk during a love scene. Put emotional intensity into your exposition while you relate the pertinent information. Give information during times of crisis, for example, when a child is arrested, a woman is revealed as a thief, or a man loses his job.

The description and action are also known as the business of your script. The business includes all the actions of the characters and the descriptions of the setting. Writing the business of your script is important, and if it is too long and boring, you'll lose the reader's interest. This is not the time to try your hand at novel writing. You need to keep the business short and to the point. Don't give elaborate explanations or descriptions. Save the flowery descriptions for your novel.

Today in the entertainment industry, writers are more concerned with their scripts being a good read than they were in the past. Whatever you do, don't have your exposition sound like a lecture. Make it so dramatic and interesting that your audience won't even be aware they are receiving information. Write with power and passion.

Sitcoms

The word *sitcom* is short for the most popular type of show on television—the situation comedy. Sitcoms usually revolve around the same characters each week. These characters either work together—as they do in such comedies as—*Taxi, News Radio, Cheers,* and *Designing Women*—or they live together as families, the most popular type of sitcom. Let's face it, there are no new plots under the sun. There are only characters who make a sitcom stand out from all the rest. Just look at the success of *Seinfeld.* It almost has no plot, yet the popularity of the unique and quirky characters have made it a success. Viewers love visiting George, Elaine, Kramer, and Jerry to see what nonissues they'll be discussing each week. They aren't the same tired, clichéd characters you see on most sitcoms.

Today, there are new versions of the family sitcom, with very different types of families. Some use characters who are divorced, single parents, or people living with relatives. Some very successful sitcoms center around friendships. Other sitcoms are centered around a successful stand-up comic who plays the lead character.

In 1996, over fifty new sitcoms appeared on television. The attrition rate is high, and some are lucky to last a month.

The best way to begin writing a spec sitcom script is to study the show or shows you want to write for. Learn everything there is to know about the characters, inside and out. Discover their foibles, fears, and frustrations by studying past scripts and diligently watching the show every week. You can purchase episodes from stores that specialize in selling scripts. (Refer to the sources.) Nobody is going to buy an episode of a sitcom that has already been made.

Most sitcoms have staff writers who write most of the episodes, with a very few going to free-lancers. So your sitcom probably won't be bought, but it *will* show whether you know the characters and can write dialogue and create a plot. Your spec sitcom will also demonstrate your ability to construct the proper form for your sitcom, using the correct format.

You should write several sitcoms for different shows to serve as examples of your writing style, not to sell. Each sample script is to show producers and agents that you are able to capture the essence of a show's characters and create an exciting and fresh plot.

Some sitcoms are considered high comedy, a sophisticated, more intellectual type of humor. Other sitcoms are referred to as low comedy, in which a lot of the humor comes from pratfalls, mistaken identity, and physical humor.

What makes one sitcom series succeed while others fail? It is the characters. How many variations on a typical sitcom can you have? Let's talk about the most popular type of sitcom, the family. Besides the traditional mother, father, and 2.5 kids, there's the single-parent-with-kids sitcom. Then there is the combined family, with two divorced or widowed parents who marry each other and then have more children together. You get the idea.

What qualities distinguish an outstanding sitcom from a mediocre one? The difference is *not* in the makeup of the family but in the makeup of the individual characters. Are they unique, original, sympathetic? Do you like them, identify with them, and root for them when they're in trouble?

Some comedy writers are great joke tellers. They know how to set up a joke and make it pay off. If that isn't your forte, don't worry, because many shows have writers who do nothing but "pump up" a script with jokes. (The average used to be three jokes on a page, but now it's even more.)

After you have studied the sitcom market and chosen the ones you want to write for, you need to write a solid script, properly structured, with a beginning, a middle, and an end, in which the major characters learn something new about themselves.

The Log Line

Study *TV Guide* or the television listings in your local newspaper to see how the description of the episode for that week is written. This is called the "log line."

The log line is the essence of the idea from which you build an entire sitcom. Your ideas must be fresh and original and not duplicate what has already been written.

The Title Page

Your title page should be approximately three inches from the top, with the name of the series, centered, in caps and underlined. Type the title of your episode in upper and lower case, enclosed in quotation marks and centered, about seven or eight spaces below the series name. "Written by" should precede your name and is positioned about an inch below the episode title, written in upper and lower case and centered.

The Sitcom Script

"ACT ONE," in capital letters and underlined, begins your script. Skip two spaces, and directly beneath it type "SCENE ONE" folled by a colon. Next, type "EXT." for "exterior" or "INT." for "interior," the location, and whether it's "DAY" or "NIGHT" or "LATER," all in caps. For example, you would write:

ACT ONE

SCENE ONE:

INT. DEN - MORNING

All dialogue is double-spaced and written in upper and lower case. One page of a sitcom is equal to thirty seconds. Your entire script should consist of forty to fifty pages.

Your margins for the action should be set at 17 and 50. The character's name is centered at 38. The dialogue is set at 25 and 60. Everything is in capital letters except the dialogue and the stage directions.

There are two acts in a sitcom, with three or four scenes in each act. It's important to do your homework and see how the sitcom you want to write for times commercial breaks. You must end each act with "<u>FADE OUT</u>," written in caps and underlined. You also use caps and an underline for "<u>TAG</u>" and "<u>THE END</u>."

The sitcom structure differs from a television movie or screenplay in that the dialogue is double-spaced and everything but the dialogue and stage directions is typed in capital letters.

Hour Episodic Drama

The hour episodic dramas are one-hour shows that have a continuing cast of characters. *ER, Chicago Hope, NYPD Blue,* and *Law and Order,* all fall into the category of episodic drama.

To write a spec script for an episodic drama, begin by watching the show you've chosen until you know the characters inside and out. Make certain your own is fresh and original while conforming to the show's format. You should also know about the TV characters' past lives, as well as their current problems.

Episodic shows depend on audience allegiance to the continuing cast of characters. If you are going to write for this genre, the most important obligation you have is to create a story that actively involves the continuing cast and doesn't focus on a guest star. The biggest mistake beginning writers make is to write an episode for the guest star or stars and ignore the continuing actors. Even if your story is interesting and exciting, you won't sell it if it doesn't focus on the show's regular cast.

It's a big challenge to take a cast of characters that someone else has created and provide a story that is fresh, realistic, contemporary, and novel. You can achieve this by inventing interesting situations and problems and by bringing the human condition and current social issues to your script.

Hour dramas are written in four acts for network television and usually for cable, too. Most shows also have a teaser or hook in the beginning.

The teaser asks the question that will be answered by the end of the episode. In some hour dramas, the teaser is a recap of what happened the previous week. Sometimes a teaser provides the atmosphere of the show, reminding the television audience that they have come home.

An episode is usually between fifty-two and fifty-eight pages, sometimes fewer. An hour drama has the same script format as a screenplay, with single-spaced dialogue. You have to know if the show you're writing for is action oriented or filled with dialogue.

The duration of each of the four acts is determined by the commercial breaks. Each act runs about twelve minutes each, roughly equal parts.

Don't look down on television and say, "This is just TV." Some of the best writers are television writers. They write hour dramas of high-quality craftsmanship that deal with meaningful issues.

Features and Television Movies

Writing a spec script for a TV movie or feature film is usually easier than writing for episodic television. This is because you're free to write what you want and to create your own characters. You probably will know the characters in your screenplay intimately, because they have been born through your imagination.

When you write a feature or a TV film, your main character has an arc—a growth experience that is usually completed by the end of the drama. In contrast, characters in hour dramas usually remain the same from one week to the next.

Even in a feature film, whose viewers are in the dark in a closed theater, you have to hook the audience immediately. Most people will give you ten to fifteen minutes to grab their interest before they walk out. You don't have even that long to engage them in a TV movie. You must get the television viewer's attention immediately and hold it until the movie is over. This takes mastery of your craft, and you have to be absolutely at the top of your skills to accomplish this difficult task.

Television movies have the added challenge of commercial breaks, making it even more difficult to hold viewers' attention.

You can see why in writing for television you need to do something really powerful at these act breaks to bring your audience back, so they won't change the channel or go to another room, or worse yet, turn of the TV. You accomplish this by giving them cliffhangers, putting the characters in physical and emotional jeopardy. The strongest cliffhanger should occur at the end of the first act, because that's your setup.

Your spec script is your calling card. Make your product the best you can create. Rewrite your script until it's terrific, with exciting, multidimensional characters and a good strong story line. A well-crafted script will open many doors, so be ready, willing, and able when the opportunity for success presents itself.

Computer Programs for Scripts

There are computer programs for scriptwriters that put your script into the correct format. Some popular programs are:

Scriptware (Windows & DOS)

Final Draft (Mac)

Scriptor (Mac & IBM)

Movie Master (IBM)

Scriptthing (IBM)

Script Wizard (IBM)

CHAPTER NINE

Script Writing Part II: From Plays to Videos

"Writing is a lonely life, but the only life worth living."

—*Gustave Flaubert*

This chapter deals with the many opportunities there are for writers of scripts other than feature films or television shows.

Documentaries

One of the largest of the alternative film and video markets is that of documentaries. The federal government alone produces millions of dollars' worth of educational and instructional videos. This industry employs writers and producers from inside and outside the ranks of government.

It is difficult to obtain a steady job as a documentary writer. Because there is a better market for completed films than there is for scripts, writers must often pursue funding from various sources, such as retail enterprises that could benefit from the exposure of their product.

The best-known sources of documentary funding are the National Endowment for the Arts and the National Endowment for the Humanities. However, competition for their limited funds is intense.

Many projects are first produced by local television stations, especially public TV stations. It is possible to take your well-researched idea to a local PBS station and see it realized there.

Game Shows

Game-show writers create games, write the host's questions, and embellish contestants' answers. They also write descriptions of the prizes on the shows. They are often hired as "researchers" to foil the Writers Guild of America.

New writers are usually interviewed and given a writing assignment. Ads are sometimes placed in entertainment trade magazines by game shows seeking writers.

Radio

Although one hears a lot of patter, there are very few writers who specialize in radio. Announcers and talk-show hosts usually write their own material; commercials are written by advertising companies; and stations, such as National Public Radio, usually buy shows that are already produced. However, NPR does specialize in broadcasting news, and during the last ten years the news programs have tripled their audience, from three million to nine million. The same guidelines for writing news for other markets apply to writing radio news. The writing must be crisp, clear, and conversational, in addition to being thoroughly researched.

Daytime Dramas

In the hierarchy of a daytime drama, the executive producer, who is often also the creator, is at the top. Next is the producer, who is also often the head writer and frequently the cocreator, and who supervises the writing staff. The writing staff includes the breakdown writer, who prepares scene outlines, and the associate writers, who turn the breakdowns into dialogue.

As for opportunities for new writers on daytime dramas, the good news is that the producers look for replacement writers all year long. The bad news is that the burnout rate is extremely high. The pace is exhausting. Soap-opera writers are not always represented by agents. It is best to write a few scenes for the show you wish to work on and develop a contact on that show to get your scenes read.

Don't try to write for daytime drama without first familiarizing yourself with a specific show. The ongoing plots have continuing characters who become involved with intrigue, emotional relationships, and love. You have to know who is in love with whom and what are the latest plot twists and turns. If you're interested in writing for this market, you can find out more by reading magazines dealing with these dramas.

The following are a few of the magazines available:

Soap Opera Digest
45 West Twenty-fifth Street
New York, New York 10010

Soap Opera Weekly
41 West Twenty-fifth Street
New York, New York 10010

Animation

There are opportunities for the animation writer beyond cartoons. Animation is used in features, prime-time specials, children's TV shows, industrial and educational films, music videos, network promos, and computer graphics. On the down side, large studios, such as Disney, no longer accept unsolicited material (that is, material not submitted through an agent). One should try calling the smaller studios to get a foot in the door of the animation industry.

Plays

> "The great thing about writing: Stay with it . . . ultimately you
> teach yourself something very important about yourself."
>
> —*Bernard Malamud*

Writers are attracted to play writing for the live interaction between actors and the audience. Plays can range from the ten-minute play, which has become very popular, to the one-act and the full-length, two-act play. Think of the one-act play as you would a short story, which usually deals with a single idea. A two-act is more like a novel, with each act broken up into scenes.

A good starting point for your adventure in writing plays is the ten-minute play. In writing a ten-minute play, you are writing about a moment in time. There is even a major ten-minute-play contest held in Louisville, Kentucky.

There is an immediacy in a play that television does not have. The audience is sharing the same space with the actors and experiencing their actions as they are happening. In film or television, the camera creates an atmosphere through close-ups or long shots.

Since there isn't a camera to interpret a play, the actors are dependent on dialogue and actions. Though dialogue is of prime importance, you can't solely depend on it. You also need action, gestures, and movement. You want your dialogue combined with actions, so you don't end up with talking heads on the stage.

Have a reading of your play, so you can hear how it sounds. Record it, and afterward have an audience-participation discussion, where your play is critiqued. It's best to have a few writers in the audience who will give you valuable information on what's working and what's not. Get actors to read the parts and listen to their feedback on whether the dialogue was awkward or easy to read.

My first play had a cast of fourteen characters. I soon found out that theaters prefer a cast of four to six characters at the most. Think about the economics of paying a huge cast of fourteen actors and you'll understand why.

Agents for Playwrights

Most agents for plays are in New York. They usually won't consider your play unless you've been fortunate enough to have had a production. So it's almost like getting into a union or a guild—you can't get in until you have credits, and yet many people won't hire you if you aren't in the union. So what to do? Be vigilant, persistent, and tenacious. Everyone who's made it had to start at the beginning. Don't get discouraged. Forge ahead with a belief in yourself and in your work.

To learn more about what role an agent will play in your career as a playwright, you can write for a free booklet from the Society of Authors' Representatives. (For further information, see the appendix.)

Another way to find an agent is to network with other playwrights. Get personal referrals of agents they know and like, and find out what kinds of plays they represent.

Resources for Playwrights

The Dramatists Guild publishes a wonderful sourcebook for playwrights. You don't have to be a produced playwright to join this helpful organization. You may join as an associate member. This is an excellent way to learn about the field and to receive current information on contests and grants. The sourcebook also contains a list of contacts for marketing your play.

Grants for playwrights are available from both public and private organizations. The National Endowment for the Arts gives grants to professional playwrights. For information see the appendix.

Look into your local, regional, and state government agencies. Often they will offer individual grants to residents in their area. Check out your community arts council to see if it offers any programs, and send for lists of grants and foundations compiled by your state's cultural and arts agencies.

Marketing Plays

Marketing a play is very similar to marketing a novel. You need to write an exciting query letter, include reviews of your play if it has been produced, and a synopsis of no more than ten pages.

Don't hold out for an opening on Broadway—that's a rare occurrence. Try to get your play produced in a local or regional theater. Then you can build up a portfolio of reviews, newspaper articles, and any other type of publicity your play receives. These will become your press kit.

Good reviews at a local theater often lead to productions of your play at larger regional theaters. If the reviews are terrific, your play may be invited to a national or international play festival.

Play Writing Contests and Awards

When you enter your play in a contest or send it to a publisher or a grant committee, you must have it typed in the correct format and include a self-addressed, stamped envelope. Before you send out your play, make certain you have followed the organization's guidelines for submission. Some contests require an entry fee. For more information, refer to the appendix.

Interactive Media

There is a large and growing market for interactive-media material. Interactive programs allow the user to control the narrative at many different points in the story. The medium has both educational and entertainment value and is an effective teaching tool.

The demands of interactive writing are different from those of linear storytelling. An interactive story changes with each retelling. It is not linear but fluid. It has an almost infinite combination of beginnings, middles, and endings.

The interactive media market is growing at an accelerated rate. If you want to be a writer in the interactive market, you must educate yourself. Rent videos and study them as you would novels or films. You can also read magazines and books about interactive media. More and more there are markets opening up for interactive media. Some of them include: Big business, education, entertainment, and training. These markets have found the interactive media to be an effective teaching tool. A particularly good book on the subject is *Demystifying Multimedia,* by Rand Haykinin. You might also contact the International Interactive Communications Society, an organization for people interested in interactive multimedia at 10160 S.W. Nimbus Ave., Suite F2, Portland, Oregon 97223, (503) 620-3604.

CHAPTER TEN

Journal Writing: From Journals to Memoirs

"Inside myself is a place where I live all alone, and that's where you renew your springs that never dry up."

—*Pearl S. Buck*

Journal writing is for anyone interested in self-exploration and personal growth. This type of writing enables you to open the door to unfinished business, blocked emotions, and repressed feelings. "Journaling" enables individuals to try out new behavior in the safety of the page. You don't need an instruction book on how to keep a journal. It is something you can do instinctively without formal training.

Writing in a journal is a good way to connect with your intuitive and spiritual self. It allows you to mine your inner resources, and to reach inside to your private self and get acquainted with the real you.

The Personal Journal

"One's own self is well hidden from one's own self."

—Friedrich Nietzsche

This type of journaling is a wonderful way to connect to your inner self and your inner wisdom. It also allows you to record your external life and relationships.

A personal journal allows you to monitor your emotional self on a daily, weekly, or monthly basis. Your feelings are the real barometer of who you are and what you're about.

When you keep a journal or diary, it's a good idea to get in the daily habit of writing. Writing in your journal on a regular basis helps you understand yourself and leads to personal growth and empowerment. There are many ways to write in a journal. When I teach journal-writing workshops, I tell students to have their journal with them at all times. You don't have to go out and buy a large, expensive journal, because you'll probably never take it with you or have it when you need it. I suggest using a small notebook that can fit in a pocket or pocketbook.

You can work on your personal problems through writing about them in your journal. And you'll often discover solutions to these current problems, through your journal.

There will be times when you'll think you don't have anything to write about. At such times, just let your mind free-associate, and write about whatever images or feelings come up. Open yourself to all the creative potential that resides within you.

Here are some basic instructions for writing in your journal:

1. Never worry about grammar, spelling, or punctuation.

2. After you start writing, don't stop for any reason. Don't edit or rewrite, but just keep writing until you're finished.

3. Set aside a specific amount of time—at least twenty minutes a day—for your writing, and don't stop before the time is up.

4. Get comfortable and relaxed before you start to write. Allow yourself privacy, with no interruptions.

5. Sometimes it's a good idea to play classical music or any music that you find relaxing. The music shuts out distractions and noise.

6. If you get stuck and feel you can't write, then write about your feelings in the moment.

The Writer's Journal

"When one is a stranger to oneself then one is estranged from others too."

—*Anne Morrow Lindberg*

A writer should master the practice of self-observation. Every encounter, event, and action should be material for your writing. Use your journal to write down ideas for future and present projects.

Take your journal with you wherever you go, and when you overhear an exciting conversation in the bank, beauty parlor, or beer hall, write it in your notebook. You are honing your awareness of human behavior. When you observe an interesting character, notice the quirks or idiosyncrasies he or she has and note them in your journal.

Writing in your journal will help you become more aware that writing is not only the act of putting words on paper, but also a full-time process of germinating ideas, concepts, characters, and plots. Your journal will be your companion, enabling you to work on your writing projects even when you're not.

The Dream Journal

"Many characters have come to me . . . in a dream. I always write down all my dreams."

—*William Burroughs*

Dream journals are a good source of stories. Keep your dream journal by your bedside with a pencil or pen. Immediately upon awakening, write down your dream, or it will somehow vanish into thin air with your first cup of coffee. Get in the habit of recording your dreams, even if you can't remember most of them. In time, you will recall them in more detail. Your dreams express your feelings, hopes, and fears. Several writers I have worked with have successfully turned their dreams into scripts and novels.

Transforming Personal Stories into Fiction and Nonfiction

"Write from experience and experience only."

—*Henry James*

Transforming personal experiences into fiction is a way to write your truth, your passion. In turning your memories into well-structured stories that move others, you will push your writing beyond ordinary to extraordinary.

When you write from this powerful source, you will be able to create fresh stories and original characters that come alive. This free writing allows you to explore your unconscious. Using your childhood stories as material will improve your writing.

I have worked with several screen-writing students who were required to make short films for their final project and couldn't think of anything to write. By giving them a journal assignment about their childhood, I helped them discover the subject for their short film. Instead of looking on the outside for a story, they learned how to mine the treasure within. In fact, a few of their films won prizes at film festivals, because of their personal and emotional impact. This was a result of using the journal as a pathway.

In a workshop that I conducted for women writers, one of the participants, a successful television writer, got in touch with childhood pain and her parents' relationship. She took the germ of the idea about her family and developed it into a successful feature film.

Your journal is the springboard to exciting stories that nobody but you can write.

Besides being a marvelous storage house for fiction, your journal can be the foundation for personal articles, essays, and autobiography. By making a habit of writing in your journal in a free and effortless manner, without personal censorship or self-consciousness, you are exploring your inner world and sharing your spirit and imagination with others.

I can't count the number of times that I worked with individual writers, who were either stuck on a project or blocked and couldn't think of anything to write, only to discover a wealth of stories from the subsequent journal writing exercises I created for them.

The saying "Write what you know," really makes sense if you look upon it in relation to your inner self and your personal experiences. These stories are powerful, because they not only have a "ring of truth," but they are fresh and original.

Memoirs and Autobiography

"Those who cannot remember the past are condemned to repeat it."

—George Santayana

Many people want to write down their memories to leave to their descendants. Their experiences may be written in the form of an autobiography or memoir. A memoir is a wonderful gift to give your family. You don't have to make it elaborate or write it in any specific manner.

Perhaps you want to write only about a particular time in your life. Some people write about how they have overcome an illness. Others write about a great love.

If you aren't sure what you want to include, you can start your memoir or your autobiography in a chronological way, writing about events as they occurred historically in your life. The structure of your piece would be time.

Another way to write is by dealing with the major events in your life—birth, marriage, divorce, death, moving, jobs, college—in terms of how they affected you and your family. Or you can write about events or relationships in the order of their importance to you. You don't always have to worry about a time line, and don't get hung up on worrying about the precise continuity of events. You can have the freedom to go back and forth in your past as you prod your memories. What is important is how you felt about these events. Were you angry, scared, happy, or depressed? How did what happen affect you? What caused you to make the choices that you made?

Think of Robert Frost's poem "The Road Not Taken," and maybe that will help you to explain the crossroads in your life. By writing about your past you will often relive events that had significance for you and made an impact on your personality.

Make your writing conversational and to the point. Write as if you're sitting at the dining-room table over dinner, talking to someone in your family and telling him or her about your past. Not only will your descendants have a remembrance of their heritage, but they also will have validation of their background.

I have worked with many writers who aren't interested in selling their writing but want to leave their memoirs to their children and grandchildren. In many cases, they have self-published their work and have given their books out as gifts to family members. Others have decided to share their story with friends as well as family. Still others decide to self-publish because they feel they have something important to share with the world—about overcoming great odds, perhaps, or about a moment in history. Before you decide to self-publish, ask yourself whether you are doing so in order to share your work with friends and family or as a money-making venture.

Self-Publishing

If your motives for self-publishing are more professional than personal, you need to get a better understanding of what it's all about.

When I decided to self-publish a writing book, based on more than a decade of teaching writing workshops, I had no idea what I was getting into. So I took a course on self-publishing, hoping to prepare myself. Unfortunately, the class dealt more with what type size or paper weight to use, rather than the nuts and bolts of self-publishing. I came away ignorant of such areas as distribution, bookkeeping, advertising, delivery, storage, collecting monies, and mail order.

Problems occur when you enter into self-publishing thinking you'll make lots of money. Before you leap into the world of self-publishing, ask yourself the following questions:

1. Who is the target audience for my book?

2. How much of an initial investment will I have to make to publish my book?

3. How will people learn about my book?

4. How will I make back my investment and make money?

5. Who will distribute my book?

6. Who will do the billing and collecting of monies?

7. Who will deliver my books, and how will I ship them?

These are just a few of the questions you need to answer before you self-publish. When I published my book, I had a built-in market, because I used my book as the text for the writing courses I taught. And from word of mouth, more people wanted to buy my book, so I got it into bookstores. That's when I learned about billing, deliveries, payments, discount, marketing, collecting the money, and shipping. What had started as a personal goal, to share my writing techniques with my students, suddenly erupted into a career. I had to name my company and announce it by putting my DBA (doing business as) in the local newspaper. Next I had to get a resale number so that I could sell my book to bookstores. Surprise, surprise: I now had to charge the state sales tax and keep tax records.

I'm not writing this to discourage you. I just want to share how complicated self-publishing can be. On the upside, my book gave me more credibility and opened up new opportunities as a writing instructor. I was offered a position at a local university. But remember that I had a ready-made market for my book. Do you? If the answer is yes, then go for it.

When I published, I used desktop publishing, writing on my computer, and printing my book on my letter-quality laser jet printer. I decided to use spiral binding instead of perfect binding, because I wanted the book to lie flat, so my students could use it as a workbook.

The problem with a spiral-bound book is that you can't put the title on the binding, and many bookstores will refuse to buy a book that can't be put vertically on a shelf. It takes up too much valuable space in a bookstore when it is placed face up.

It's important to decide how much you want to spend on publishing costs and storage space up front. Having my original manuscript photocopied, a hundred copies at a time, allowed me to keep the initial costs down and to have enough room to store the books.

To make a perfect-bound book cost-effective, you usually have to print at least a thousand. Of course, the more you have printed, the lower the cost per book. But do you have storage space for these books?

There are some excellent companies that specialize in printing books, but you must do your research. Avoid so-called vanity presses. The costs are very high and the only one who will end up making money will be the vanity press.

If you do self-publish, you will want to get an ISBN (International Standard Book Number). Every published book is assigned an ISBN to help with billing, ordering, and shipping. For the proper forms, send your title page, including your name and address, to R.R. Bowker, 121 Chenlon Road, New Providence, New Jersey 07974.

CHAPTER ELEVEN

The Business of Business Writing: From Technical Writing to Public Relations

"You can't go around saying you're a writer if no one will take you seriously."

—*William Kennedy*

There are many job opportunities for writers in business and industry. They include public relations, promotion, marketing, and advertising.

Technical writers are needed to write about the growing multimedia phenomena. Such writers take highly technical materials and make them understandable to lay readers. The following positions in business and industry offer possibilities for employment as a writer.

Business Writing

Many corporations have their own publications and their own advertising and promotion departments. Areas within companies where writers can find employment include training and advertising departments. Projects might include sales manuals, technical writing, brochures, newsletters, scripts, bulletins, press releases for new products, and in-house manuals.

A good source of information about what positions are available in this area is *The Standard Directory of Advertisers,* published by the National Register Publishing Company, 3004 Glenview Road, Wilmette, Illinois 60091.

Tips for Good Business Writing

"Good writing excites me, and makes life worth living."

—*Harold Pinter*

Whether you are writing reports, letters, brochures, pamphlets, or educational or informational material, it is best to be brief and to the point. Put yourself in your reader's place and ask yourself if you would be interested in what you have just written. Do you understand the content? Are you getting the point of the writing? Is the writing clear? Is it interesting? Logical? Focused?

Organize your thoughts and ideas *before* you start to write. Can you state the basic thesis or premise of your writing? What is your purpose? Do you want to persuade your reader? Convince? Sell? Educate? Inform?

Next, develop some type of outline to organize your ideas. It can be as simple as stating your most important points in a sentence or two. If you want to be more detailed, you can create the type of outline you were taught in high school, using Roman numerals for key topics, as in the following example.

I. Ice skating

    A. Rinks

    B. Ice charades

    C. Contests

  1. Olympic

      (a) couples

      (b) men skaters

      (c) women skaters

If you're a writer for a corporation, you need to know who is your audience. Are you writing a training manual for employees or supervisors? Are you writing a product brochure for customers? Are you writing a business plan for potential buyers? Are you writing a systems and procedures manual for management? Or are you writing an annual report for stockholders of the company?

Why is this important to know? Because your audience will determine what information you'll include. If you want stockholders to have confidence in the company, you'll write a positive, optimistic report. I have read glowing annual reports for companies that were losing money and customers and whose stock was going down. And yet, according to the report, these were just temporary setbacks on the road to success. Why? Because the report was focused on the positives, whatever they were, and played down the negatives. It takes a well-organized, creative writer to do the job.

Journalism

Getting a job with a newspaper is very difficult, because there are so few permanent positions for staff writers. You must be competitive and a self-starter to land one of these coveted jobs.

To be a reporter for a newspaper or the electronic media requires more than writing skill. A good writer not only conveys information but brings a story to life. Good writing is clear, free of jargon, simple, vivid, and accurate. You also must be a good generator of story ideas, and you must be productive, sometimes writing two or more stories a day.

I once worked with a young man who had received his master's degree in international relations and decided he didn't want to pursue a career in government. He wanted to become a journalist. He was a good writer, and his background helped him as a reporter. But he had to pay his dues and worked for many small newspapers in obscure places for a meager salary just to get the experience. In less than five years he had become a successful free-lancer in Europe. His stories have been published in all the major newspapers in the United States and Europe.

Since he hadn't gone to journalism school and told me that journalism school is not the only road to a career in journalism, I asked him to share what qualities he felt make a good reporter. He related the following tips:

1. Show, don't tell.

2. Keep it simple.

3. Let language paint a picture.

4. Give the story a sense of immediacy.

5. Use quotes sparingly—and only if they add punch.

6. Gather far more information than you use.

Some newspapers accept articles from free-lance writers who work on specific assignments. Pick a newspaper you would like to write for and study its format, style, and content before you submit an article. You should also send a writing sample or clips if you have any, along with a query letter. This is a good way to break into reporting. Even if you receive little or no pay, you'll be building up your portfolio.

Publicity Writing and Public Relations

There are many positions in public relations and publicity writing for community service organizations, libraries, hospitals, government agencies, and civic organizations. These areas of writing usually have to do with promoting a person, place, project, political position, point-of-view, or product. Writers develop press kits, marketing pieces, newsletters, and feature articles in the print media. They also get spot announcements on television or radio.

These are very competitive fields of writing, and you must know the competition and what's available in the job market. A good source of PR firms is *O'Dwyer's Directory of Public Relations Firms*, published by J.R. O'Dwyer, 271 Madison Avenue, New York, New York 10016.

Press Releases

A press release is a good way to get free advertising, if a newspaper will publish it. Since press releases are considered straight news stories and space to print them is limited, it's important that yours be well-written.

No matter how good your release is, however, don't depend on it alone to spread the word about your workshop, your store opening, or your newly published book. You might want to advertise as well.

Whatever your strategy, you must master the craft of making straight news concise and interesting. That way, perhaps you can beat out the thousands of other press releases vying for limited space.

You need to hook your readers immediately, because you only have a little space to get your message across. Your lead sentence needs to be especially interesting. Then you need to continue to give information in descending order of importance.

In the case of a press release, less is more. Follow your interesting and informative lead with a synopsis of the facts concerning your event—the date, time, and place. At this point, you should have succeeded in catching the editor's attention.

Get to know the editors you'll be sending your press releases to. The more personal the relationship, the better your chances of having your releases published, assuming they are well-written and newsworthy and follow the publication's guidelines.

The format of a press release is quite basic, and you can create it on your computer, using 1.5-inch margins on all sides.

As the contact person, you should type your name and address in the upper left-hand corner. Also include a phone number. Centered in bold type and underlined are the words "For Immediate Release." You may want to title your release. If you do, the title should be placed between the address and the body. It should be in caps, underlined, and single-spaced. The body of the release should start a third of the way down the page. The body should be double-spaced, with the paragraphs indented. Try to keep your release on one page, but if you can't, then type the word "more," centered at the bottom of the page, and place dashes on either side of it.

You may end your press release by using the symbol # centered at the end of your release or the number 30 enclosed in dashes or quotation marks.

For further information, contact the Public Relationships Society of America, 33 Irving Place, New York, New York 10003; (212) 995-2230.

Advertising Writing

Many businesses and corporations have in-house ad agencies that write copy and lay out ads for the company. Entry-level positions are usually low-paying and consist of very little writing. Beginners perform mostly clerical chores, such as filing, typing, and proof-reading. Nowadays, being computer literate is a plus in getting one of these entry-level jobs. After all, it's about supply and demand, and this field is inundated with thousands of college graduates who want to break into journalism or advertising.

If you are interested in breaking into the field of advertising, a good source of information is the trade magazine *Broadcasting.* There is also the National Association of Broadcasters, located at 1771 North Street, NW, Washington, D.C. 20036.

Get your foot in the door by landing any job you can with an advertising or media company. Then you'll be in position to move up when there's an opening for a copywriter, media writer, or infomercial writer.

Jobs in advertising and the media are listed in the classified sections of *Adweek* and *Mediaweek* magazines.

There are also organizations for advertising writers: For more information about writing careers in the field of advertising, contact the American Advertising Federation, 1400 K Street, NW, Suite 1000, Washington, D.C. 20005. You may also write to the Advertising Club of New York, 155 East Fifty-fifth Street, Suite 202, New York, New York 10022.

Commercials

If you wish to become a writer of commercials and other promotional material, your best bet is to affiliate yourself with an advertising agency. Trailers, which are commercials for motion pictures, are usually handled by the distribution company, which hires writers known to them. If you are able to get into a company that writes and produces trailers, you will also have an opportunity to learn about filmmaking on a small scale.

Another source of information is the trade magazine *Broadcasting*. If you would like a list of broadcasters to contact, send a self-addressed, stamped envelope with your request to the National Association of Broadcasters, 1771 North Street, NW, Washington, D.C. 20036.

Now that you are more aware of what jobs are out there, you need to discover who the players are in the writing market. The following chapter will provide you with all the information you need.

CHAPTER TWELVE

The Writer's Market: From Networks to Publishers

"You can't want to be a writer, you have to be one."

—*Paul Theroux*

When you submit your writing, you first need a plan. Research the companies you want to send your script to. If you've written a science-fiction script and the production company or movie studio makes nothing but action adventures, forget it—you don't stand a chance. If you've written a romance novel, don't send your work to a publishing house that only publishes horror fiction. To find the right publisher, go to the public library or a bookstore and pick up a copy of *Writer's Market*. It lists the names and address of book and magazine publishers, the type of material they're looking for, and how much they pay, and gives guidelines on how to prepare your manuscript.

A word of caution: Always call the publisher and ask for the name of an editor to send your manuscript to. Positions change quickly, and you certainly don't want to handicap yourself from the beginning by using the name of an editor who is no longer with the company. Nothing is as sweet to editors' ears as the sound of their own name, so be certain to get it right.

If you get a rejection, don't take it personally! *All it means is that your product is not what the company is buying at the moment.* File away the rejection, and put another manuscript into the mail. And don't stop submitting. Believe in your work and know that it has merit.

Many successful screenwriters never sold their first script until *after* they sold their third and fourth scripts.

The following sections explain what the markets are for writers in the entertainment business.

Networks

Network television offers the greatest diversity of writing jobs within the entertainment industry. As a TV newswriter, you might write news stories, continuity pieces, introductions, descriptions, or narrative copy to be used by an anchorperson.

In the on-air promotion department, a writer/producer writes the copy and supervises the editing of announcements promoting upcoming shows and the network itself.

If you are hired as a public relations and marketing writer, you write press releases and establish relationships with reporters for the various media in order to obtain coverage for the network.

On the more creative side, game shows are entirely scripted by staff writers. Episodic television dramas and sitcoms hire both staff and free-lance writers to craft their stories; daytime dramas and variety shows employ staff writers only.

Made-for-TV movies are contracted with writers on an individual basis, generally requiring the use of an agent as an intermediary. Children's programming, including cartoons and animation, uses both staff and free-lance writers.

The following are addresses of networks:

ABC Entertainment   (310) 557-7777
2040 Avenue of the Stars
Los Angeles, California 90067-4785

CBS Entertainment   (213) 852-2345
7800 Beverly Boulevard
Los Angeles, California 90036-2188

NBC Entertainment   (818) 840-4444
3000 West Alameda Avenue
Burbank, California 91523-0001

Fox TV Center Productions   (213) 856-1234
5746 Sunset Boulevard
Los Angeles, California 90028-8588

PBS   (703) 739-5000
1320 Braddock Place
Alexandria, Virginia 22314

KCET   (213) 666-6500
4401 Sunset Boulevard
Los Angeles, California 90027

PBS New York   (212) 708-3000
1790 Broadway, Sixteenth Floor
New York, New York 10019

Production Companies

Production companies work with writers whose current scripts or
previous works appeal to them. They do this in order to perfect
and sell a written project to a television network, cable company,
or movie studio. The television or movie writer submits his or her
script to the production company, preferably through an agent,
and the piece is evaluated by a reader.

Some production companies are large enough to produce the project themselves with the help of a distribution company. Within production companies, there are writing jobs for creative analysts, story analysts, development directors, and script readers. Good writing and analytical skills are needed for these jobs, which can serve as door openers for writers.

The following are some of the largest production companies:

Walt Disney & Touchstone TV   (818) 560-1000
500 South Buena Vista
Burbank, California 91521-0001

Columbia Pictures   (310) 280-8000
10202 West Washington Boulevard
Culver City, California 90232-3195

Hollywood Pictures   (818) 560-1000
500 South Buena Vista Street
Burbank, California 91521-0001

Metro Goldwyn Mayer/U.A.   (310) 449-3000
2500 Broadway Street
Santa Monica, California 90404-3061

Orion Pictures   (310) 282-0550
1888 Century Park East, Seventh Floor
Los Angeles, California 90067-1728

Paramount Studios   (213) 956-5000
5555 Melrose Avenue
Los Angeles, California 90038-3197

Sony Pictures Entertainment   (310) 280-8000
10202 West Washington Boulevard
Culver City, California 90232-3195

Tristar Pictures   (310) 280-7700
c/o TriStar Building
10202 West Washington Boulevard
Culver City, California 90232-3195

Tristar TV   (310) 202-1234
1888 Century Park East
Los Angeles, California 90067

20th Century Fox   (310) 277-2211
10201 West Pico Boulevard
Los Angeles, California 90035

Universal   (818) 777-1000
100 Universal City Plaza
Universal City, California 91608-1085

Warner Brothers Studios   (818) 954-6000
4000 Warner Boulevard
Burbank, California 91522-0001

Cable

Cable organizations assemble programs on specific channels on a daily basis. The only difference between the commercial networks and cable lies in their assigned UHF frequencies. Commercial networks are assigned the frequencies between 2 and 13, and cable networks are assigned numbers above 13.

Writing opportunities closely resemble those in network television. The writer seeking employment would send his or her spec script or résumé to individual cable companies, such as Disney and Lifetime.

The following is a partial list of cable companies:

CNN Los Angeles   (213) 993-5000
6430 Sunset Boulevard, No. 300
Los Angeles, California 90028

CNN Atlanta   (404) 827-1500
1 CNN Center
P.O. Box 105366
Atlanta, Georgia 30348-5366

Comedy Central   (212) 767-8600
1775 Broadway, Tenth Floor
New York, New York 10019

Nickelodeon/Nick At Nite   (212) 258-7500
1515 Broadway, Twenty-first Floor
New York, New York 10036

Disney Channel   (818) 569-7500
3800 West Alameda Avenue
Burbank, California 91505-4398

HBO Los Angeles   (310) 201-9200
2049 Century Park East, Suite 4100
Los Angeles, California 90067-3215

HBO New York   (212) 512-1000
1100 Sixth Avenue
New York, New York 10036-6737

MTV Networks   (212) 258-8000
1515 Broadway
New York, New York 10036

Showtime Networks   (818) 505-7700
10 Universal City Plaza, Thirty-first Floor
Universal City, California 91608-1002

Turner (TBS) Los Angeles   (310) 551-6300
1888 Century Park East
Los Angeles, California 90067-3215

Syndication

Writers who work for syndication companies are largely engaged
in on-air promotion or public relations. The following is a partial
list of syndicators:

All American Communications   (310) 656-1100
808 Wilshire Boulevard
Santa Monica, CA 90401

Beck/Ola Productions   (310) 315-4715
3000 West Olympic Boulevard, Building 1
Santa Monica, California 90404

Dick Clark Productions   (818) 841-3003
3003 West Olive Avenue
Burbank, California 91510-7811

Fox Star Productions
10261 West Pico Boulevard, Building 3/3
Los Angeles, California 90035

Franklin/Waterman Entertainment
2644 Thirtieth Street, First Floor
Santa Monica, California 90405

(310) 452-9100

Harvey Famous Studios
1999 Avenue of the Stars, Suite 2050
Los Angeles, CA 90067

(310) 789-1990

Hallet Street Productions
519 North Arden Drive
Beverly Hills, California 90210-3507

(213) 874-3000

King World Productions
12400 Wilshire Boulevard, Suite 1200
Los Angeles, California 90025-1019

(310) 826-1108

Videos

Often overlooked in a search for a writing career, the field of educational and corporate video generates four times the revenue of theatrical films and television. The widespread opportunities range from large corporations, such as Westinghouse, to small, local video production houses in your neighborhood. The larger companies often have in-house production companies, but small as well as large companies often employ free-lancers. Advertising agencies also create films and utilize free-lance producers and writers.

The following is a partial list of video companies:

A & E Television Network
235 East Forty-fifth Street
New York, New York 10017

(212) 661-4500

Casablanca Productions
8544 W. Sunset Boulevard
West Hollywood, CA 90069

(310) 659-2067

DB USA
9454 Wilshire Boulevard, Penthouse 15
Beverly Hills, California 90212

(310) 278-8125

Imaginazium
15718 Milbank Street
Encino, California 91436

Jumbo Pictures
161 Sixth Avenue, Fifteenth Floor
New York, NY 10013

(212) 337-0077

Lone Star Pictures International
4826 Greenville Avenue
Dallas, Texas 75206

Media Star Entertainment
1341 Ocean Avenue, Suite 280
Santa Monica, California 90401

Metaphor Productions
1012 Tenth Street, Suite 2
Santa Monica, California 90403

New Line Productions
888 Seventh Avenue, Twentieth Floor
New York, New York 10106

(212) 649-4900

Interactive Media

The cutting edge of entertainment technology, interactive media creates videos that allow the viewer to alter the course of events in a story. This technique holds exciting possibilities for scriptwriters, who may have to meet a large and sudden demand for corporate training, educational, and business-management videos, as well as home entertainment and arcade-type programs.

The following is a partial list of companies specializing in interactive media:

Beverly Hills Producers Group   (310) 788-5511
449 South Beverly Drive, Third Floor
Beverly Hills, California 90212

Bates Entertainment   (213) 962-9204
137 North Larchmont Boulevard,
Suite 805
Los Angeles, California 90004

Cineville Inc.   (310) 394-4699
225 Santa Monica Boulevard,
Seventh Floor
Santa Monica, California 90401

El Nino Films
650 North Bronson, Suite B-140
Los Angeles, California 90004

Hart-Thomas-Berlin Productions   (212) 724-1948
200 West Eighty-sixth Street
New York, New York 10024

The Knight Company   (310) 395-7100
1337 Ocean Avenue, South Penthouse
Santa Monica, California 90401

National Lampoon   (310) 474-5252
10850 Wilshire Boulevard, Suite 1000
Los Angeles, California 90024

New Media Inc.   (203) 226-5853
One Glen Dening
Westport, Connecticut 06880

Atelier Pictures   (213) 993-7006
1438 North Gower Street, Box 26
Los Angeles, California 93422

DIC Entertainment   (818) 955-5400
303 North Glenoaks Boulevard
Burbank, California 91502

Publishing Houses

The large publishing houses have become an increasingly difficult market for the beginning writer to break into with his or her
first writing project. Unless you have personal contacts or a good
agent, it will prove less frustrating to try the smaller presses. Here
is a partial list of some of the largest publishers.

Houghton Mifflin Company
2 Park Street
Boston, Massachusetts 02108

Simon & Schuster
1230 Avenue of the Americas
New York, New York 10020

Doubleday
1540 Broadway
New York, New York 10020

Ballantine Books
201 East Fiftieth Street
New York, New York 10022

Avon Books
1350 Avenue of the Americas
New York, New York 10019

W.W. Norton & Co., Inc.
500 Fifth Avenue
New York, New York 10110

Hyperion
114 Fifth Avenue
New York, New York 10011

Magazines

There are roughly twenty-two thousand magazines published in the United States. Of these, approximately two thousand are consumer magazines, and the other 90 percent are trade, business, and professional magazines. Areas of opportunity for writers include special subjects, celebrity profiles, travel articles, trade articles, and house organs.

The following is a partial list of magazines:

Consumer Magazines

Harper's
666 Broadway, Eleventh Floor
New York, New York 10012

Parade Publications
711 Third Avenue
New York, New York 10017

Real People
950 Third Avenue, Sixteenth Floor
New York, New York 10022-2703

Saturday Evening Post
1100 Waterway Boulevard
Indianapolis, Indiana 46202

National Geographic
1145 Seventeenth Street, NW
Washington, D.C. 20036

Trade Magazines

American Health
28 West Twenty-third Street
New York, New York 10010

Coins
700 East State Street
Liola, Wisconsin 54990-0001

Popular Mechanics
224 West Fifty-seventh Street, Third Floor
New York, New York 10019

Aboard Magazine
100 Almeria, Suite 220
Coral Gables, Florida 33134

Small Presses

The smaller presses provide a good opportunity for new authors to break in. Several of the nonprofit literary presses pay modest advances and market nationally. The trick is to do your research and find the ones that specialize in your type of material.

Silver Moon Press
P.O. Box 12994
Tucson, Arizona 85732

Potential Development
40 Hazelwood Drive, Suite 101
Amherst, New York 14228-2223

E.M. Press
Box 4057
Manassas, Virginia 22110

B&B Publishing
P.O. Box 393
Fontana, Wisconsin 53125-0393

Xenos Books
Box 52152
Riverside, California 92517

Newspapers

To write for a newspaper, one generally needs a degree in journalism from an accredited college. Your best shot may be to start with a community newspaper, of which you may find several in your area. The usual newspaper hierarchy is as follows:

1. Publisher
2. Managing editor
3. Foreign editor, U.S. editor, City editor
4. Editors of various sections (sports, puzzles, style)
5. Reporters
6. Copy editors, copyreaders

The following is a partial list of newspapers:

The New York Times
229 West Forty-third Street
New York, New York 10036

Washington Post
1150 Fifteenth Street, NW
Washington, D.C. 20071

Los Angeles Times
Times Mirror Square
Los Angeles, California 90053

Daily News New York
220 East Forty-second Street
New York, New York 10017

Chicago Tribune
435 North Michigan Avenue
Chicago, Illinois 60611

Literary Journals

Literary journals provide a great service by publishing poets and fine-art writers in magazine format. Many a writer's reputation has been made by the consistent appearance of his or her work in literary magazines.

The following is a partial list of literary magazines:

The Hudson Review
684 Park Avenue
New York, New York 10021

The Paris Review
541 East Seventy-second Street
New York, New York 10021

Santa Monica Review
Santa Monica College
1900 Pico Boulevard
Santa Monica, California 90405

Yale Review
Yale University
P.O. Box 208243
New Haven, Connecticut 06520-8243

Partisan Review
Boston University
236 Bay State Road
Boston, Massachusetts 02215

Corporate Publishers

There are five thousand internal publications issued by American companies. They are mainly trade magazines such as *Ford Times*. Practically every large corporation has an in-house publications department. They are an excellent source of employment for writers, both staff and free-lance.

Educational Publishers

The writing of textbooks is usually handled by an executive editor, hired by a publisher. The executive editor hires, on a royalty basis, educators in the field as senior authors. They, in turn, hire free-lance writers to write or adapt text, poems, biography, fiction, or whatever, for textbooks. The senior author also hires editorial assistants to proofread and edit.

The following is a partial list of educational publishers:

Barron's Educational Series
250 Wireless Boulevard
Hauppauge, New York 11788

American Educational Publishing
150 East Wilson Bridge Road, Suite 145
Columbus, Ohio 43085

Social Science Education Consortium
3300 Mitchell Lane, Suite 240
Boulder, Colorado 80301-2296

Cambridge Educational Series
P.O. Box 2152
Charleston, West Virginia 25328-2153

University Presses

University presses tend to publish avant-garde and/or intellectual prose, poetry, literary criticism, and scholarly writing. University presses can be potentially useful for previously unpublished authors.

The following is a partial list of university presses:

Rutgers University Press
109 Church Street
New Brunswick, New Jersey 08901

University of California Press
2120 Berkeley Way
Berkeley, California 94720

University of Chicago Press
5801 South Ellis Avenue
Chicago, Illinois 60637

Purdue University Press
1532 Campus Courts Boulevard
West Lafayette, Indiana 47907-1532

Oregon State University Press
101 Waldo Hall
Corvallis, Oregon 97331-6407

New York University Press
70 Washington Square South
New York, New York, 10012

Syracuse University Press
1600 Jamesville Avenue
Syracuse, New York 13244

Stanford University Press
Stanford, California 94305-2235

Columbia University Press
562 West 113th Street
New York, New York 10025

Harvard University Press
79 Garden Street
Cambridge, Massachusetts 02138

Princeton University Press
41 William Street
Princeton, New Jersey 08540

Oxford University Press
200 Madison Avenue
New York, New York 10016

CHAPTER THIRTEEN

The Writing Industry: From Making Contacts to Signing Contracts

"Writing is a wholetime job . . ."

—*W. Somerset Maugham*

In the 1990s, it's more difficult than ever to be a writer. Doing business is tough, and only the most competitive and resourceful writers will survive. Publishing companies, networks, and movie studios are being bought by giant conglomerates, and there are more executives interested in the bottom line rather than creativity.

Most writers spend far more time mastering their craft than learning how to sell their work. After pouring their heart and soul into their writing, they seem to think their work will automatically be sold, and are often completely unprepared for the next step: marketing themselves and their writing in a very competitive, overcrowded marketplace. If you want to sell what you write, you must be willing to be the promoter, the marketer, and the business person in your writing career.

There are a multitude of excellent writers who have written terrific books, scripts, sitcoms, short stories, plays, and children's books, who never succeed in the writing business. This is because they fail to realize the writing process has two components—writing and selling. In this business, it's often more about who you know and less about what you know.

Writing a well-crafted, interesting piece of work alone does-n't guarantee success. To be successful as a writer, you will have to deal with business people who make decisions about your writing and your future. These decisions are often not based on the merit of the writing itself but on many other variables.

Writing is a business, and you need to apply the same princi-ples that are used in any successful business to your career. Once you are satisfied with your final product, you have to take it to the marketplace and try to sell it, just as you would a set of tires, a ream of paper, or a bushel of potatoes.

"Difficulties are things that show what men are."

—*Epictetus*

Some of the qualities you need as a business person/writer are self-discipline, self-motivation, self-promotion. You have to be a salesperson who doesn't give up and who keeps sending out your product (play, short story, novel, script, sitcom, etc.) over and over again.

As a writer, you are working for yourself, not only when you write but even more so after you've finished writing. Unless you are a staff writer for a magazine or newspaper, a television show or a corporation, you are self-employed. The selling of your product is your business. You are not only the writer, you are the manager, president, marketing person, publicist, and business manager. If it sounds difficult, that's because it is.

On the other hand, the rewards from writing can be great. Getting published, getting paid for your writing, seeing your work in print or on the screen, getting recognition, respect and fame are worth the blood sweat and tears it takes to create your product.

When you speak to an agent, an editor, or a producer on the phone or in person, it's a good idea to write out what you want to say and practice it until you sound confident discussing your project. If you pitch your story to producers or directors, practice saying your pitch into a tape recorder before your meeting. Anticipate any questions or objections so you have prepared answers. Think of the resistance you could encounter when you present your work, and have a plan to counteract it without being defensive.

Don't give in to hurt feelings or a damaged ego if people reject your work. Put your emotions aside and keep trying. Don't sit around and wait for the phone to ring or the mail to come. Keep busy!

Find out who are the decision makers and how to reach them in the organizations you target. If you are fortunate enough to get your writing project to people in the industry, here are a few tips to follow.

Since executives in decision-making positions like to think their ideas are great, don't tell them anything different when they give you suggestions. If an executive with a production company or an editor makes changes in your story, just listen and be quiet. If you want to see your script up on the big screen or your novel published, you need to get the potential buyer excited by and involved in your story. If you want to sell your writing, you'll make the changes he wants. On the other hand, if you absolutely disagree with what he's saying and under no circumstances would you make such changes, speak up. But your project will probably not get done. The writing industry is a collaborative effort, and you have to learn to be flexible.

There's a tremendous amount of money to be made in the writing industry, especially in the electronic media such as television, video, cable, films, and the Internet. The writing industry can be thought of as the last Klondike or the lottery, where a first-time screenwriter or novelist can make millions. Just look at such popular novelists as Tom Clancy, Dick Francis, John Grisham, Jackie Collins, and Danielle Steele and the screenwriters Joe Esterhas or Shane Black, who get hundreds of thousands of dollars and in some cases seven figures for just one manuscript or script.

Being successful in the writing industry and selling your script to a movie or television studio, or your articles to magazines and newspapers, or your novel to a publisher, is like being a main character in a story you wrote. You're using some of the same techniques you used in the writing of your story: setting a goal, having a destination, overcoming obstacles and complications, and reaching a climax or resolution. As a character in your writing journal, you will discover that the way to reach your goal is to *take action.* You must persist until you get the desired results.

First you must target the publishing companies, magazines, studios, or networks that you want to buy your writing. Next you have to create a plan to reach those goals. Don't wait for others to do it for you, and that includes even those of you who have an agent. It's ultimately up to you to get what you want for yourself.

The motivation to sell your script or manuscript must come from you. Your desire to write, produce, and sell your writing must come from a desire to please yourself and not someone else. Whether you will have a career as a writer can't depend upon whether someone in BCA Company liked or rejected your script. I've consulted with many writers who were about to give up because some editor or agent didn't like their writing. If your confidence can be undermined by what others think of your work, you might as well give up now, because it's just too painful to allow yourself to be at the mercy of others.

There's an old joke about a person refusing to go out with someone. A friend says, "Getting a date is like getting a cable car, there's always another one coming in ten minutes."

It's something for you to remember when you're trying to get a buyer for your writing.

Continue to send out your script or manuscript no matter what happens. If you haven't had a response after a reasonable amount of time, follow up with a phone call or a personal letter. I have often had to call or write a letter to find out the status of my script after I have sent it to a production company, studio, or agent. Since your submission is not the only one they are concerned with, you have to take the initiative, because it's certainly the only one *you're* interested in. It's up to you to follow up if you don't know what's going on.

In the writing business, you must have an unswerving belief in yourself and in your work. On the other hand, don't let your ego take over from your better judgment. If you hear the same criticism about your work over and over again, listen to it and do the necessary rewriting. If you're not certain what to do, consult a script doctor or a writing consultant! When you feel your product is absolutely the best it will ever be, it is time to stick to your guns.

If you wish to work on a TV show but can't get a job as a writer, be creative and discover what other types of jobs will give you access to the position you ultimately desire. You could be a script analyst or a reader for a production company or a network. Or you could get an entry-level job just to learn the business and to support your writing habit.

Many successful writers started out as personal assistants, secretaries, mail-room clerks, or production assistants just to be in the right place at the right time. They always had their material ready to submit.

One of my students, whom I'll call Melinda, supported her writing habit by working as a temporary secretary in the entertainment industry. Because she had excellent skills, she was offered a full-time job with ABC. She made many contacts there, and when a group of writers sold their sitcom, they asked her to work with them on the show as a writer's assistant. She took the job, sat in on meetings, took notes on every script, and in her spare time wrote a spec script for the series.

When the opportunity presented itself, she showed her script to the story editor, and because the editor was impressed with her ability to capture the essence of each character, Melinda was given an assignment. She wrote an excellent script, which led to several more assignments, and the following year she became a staff writer for another sitcom, which one of the writers cocreated and produced.

As the scout motto goes, "Be prepared." If Melinda hadn't mastered the craft and hadn't had writing samples ready, it wouldn't have mattered where she got a job. She had to have a product to sell, and she did.

I can't tell you how many times former students have called me in a panic because an opportunity presented itself and they couldn't produce. Either they didn't know how or they hadn't bothered to perfect their script to the point where it was professional enough to show anyone.

Another student worked as a secretary and met another secretary in the office. They decided to collaborate and wrote a few episodes for the show they were working on. They got so familiar with the show that some of the writers read their episodes and produced them. The two men wrote scripts for other sitcoms and eventually became staff writers on several television sitcoms.

It's up to you to make opportunities for yourself and be ready to act when they occur. Many people who seem to have had a lucky break in fact made their own luck, by being in the right place at the right time and having a sample of writing to show.

Another former writing student in her late twenties already had a high-paying job as a development executive for a major production company. Many people would have thought they had arrived once they had such a powerful position, reading scripts and developing shows for the network. She helped many writers achieve success in the television industry. But her true love was writing, and even though she worked ten to twelve hours a day, she'd awaken at five in the morning to write. While working at a full-time job, she wrote eleven scripts, some sitcoms, and episodic dramas.

Being goal-oriented, she developed a plan and took a year off to perfect her craft. She studied the market and wrote some spec scripts for several newer shows. She attended my private journal-writing workshop, which helps writers reach their emotions. Her writing improved dramatically, because after reaching inside herself, she was able to make her characters become emotionally richer.

Today she is on the staff of an hour drama and has also worked on a top sitcom. By taking one step at a time and keeping her long-term goal in sight, she has become a television writer.

Her new goal is to be a television producer of television movies, and I know that one day she will reach it because of her sense of purpose and her ability to take action and work her plan.

If you are serious about being a professional writer, then you need to treat writing as you would any job. Just as award-winning athletes master their physical skills, you too must master the skill of writing. This means putting in the time and the toil to perfect the task. Set a regular schedule for your "writing job," and go to work on a regular basis. If you work better by setting a specific time, then have a daily schedule—9 A.M. to 1 P.M., for example. The writing comes first. I have found that when a task is difficult—and writing certainly is difficult—people tend to do other things first. If you find yourself cleaning the refrigerator when you should be writing, stop, because you'll never get any writing done. Write first thing and you will have the rest of the day to do other things, such as making contacts and marketing yourself.

Marketing your book or screenplay is as much a part of the writing process as the writing itself. Set aside one or more days each week to do your marketing. Read about what's going on in the industry.

If you're a screenwriter, subscribe to *Variety, The Reporter,* or *The Hollywood Scriptwriter.* Follow the production schedules for television shows and feature films and keep a file of the producers and the production companies who make films or TV projects similar to yours. When you're ready to show your script, you will have a file ready from which to work. Working your file means calling the people in it and trying to set up an appointment to "pitch" your script or to tell them about it.

I know writers who broke into the writing business via their job as a lawyer, a nutritionist, a hairdresser, a personal trainer, a reader, and a personal assistant to a star.

There are always opportunities if you're positioned and prepared. As a writer/businessperson, you probably will develop relationships with agents, editors, publishers, producers, networks, studios, magazines, and newspapers. You will have an advantage going to do battle fully prepared and not going into it like a lamb to the slaughter.

When a publishing or production company buys your script or manuscript, it is making an investment in you and your product with the hope that it will sell. You, likewise, have spent a great deal of time, energy, and hard work in developing your product, so you want to get remunerated in the best possible way, especially since you'll have to go through this process all over again with your next project. An agent will help ensure that you get the best possible deal. If you don't have an agent and want to get one, librarians are often helpful in directing you to the proper publisher.

On the other hand, by making your own deal, you won't have to pay a commission on every royalty you receive. You should decide on the minimum that you will accept for your book or screenplay. Be prepared to walk away from a deal if you don't like the terms.

However, if your bottom line is that you want to be a published writer no matter what, you will probably accept what's offered to you. Decide on what your goal is, and be *active* in your negotiations.

One way to start your writing career is as a free-lance reader, reading manuscripts for a publishing house or scripts for a studio, then writing up an analysis. In your analysis, you critique and write up a synopsis, then recommend whether to rejct it or move it forward in the consideration process. Although this is usually an entry-level job with low pay, it is a very important one, and the experience you get is invaluable. If you learn while you're reading other people's stories what constitutes a good piece of writing and what doesn't, you'll be improving your own writing in the process.

Within the entertainment industry and the publishing business, there is a vast need for writers who handle promotional and book-jacket copy. The classified ads in *Publishers Weekly* list job openings at publishing houses. Local newspapers also occasionally advertise writing jobs. You must be a go-getter. Call the editor of the department where you'd like to work and find out if any positions are available. Be aggressive and confident.

A Writing Career

"Patience is the best remedy for every trouble."

—*Plautus*

Beginning writers often want to know if they should move to New York or Los Angeles to make contacts that will help them sell their writing. This would be ideal. In New York you could be near all the magazine and book publishers. If you're a screen or television writer, Los Angeles is the hotbed of activity for production companies, networks, independent producers, and directors. It is the hub for all types of scriptwriters. Both locations have the top agents in their particular writing fields.

There are obvious advantages in being near studios, production companies, and networks. You can meet people, get an entry-level job, and work your way up the ladder. You can keep up with what's new and what's hot. In Hollywood, more often than not it's who you know that gets your script read. But the bottom line is that you have to write, and you can write in Minneapolis, Pittsburgh, or wherever you live. First comes the need to develop not just one script but many, not just one article but a portfolio.

A career in writing is like having on-the-job training. You have no regular paycheck, no supervisor urging you to get your work done. You need to be a marketer, a manager, an efficiency expert, a self-starter, and a cheerleader. You especially need to be good in managing your time. You must follow a self-imposed writing schedule until it becomes a habit.

When you start to send out your material to publishers or agents, don't wait until someone sends your query letter back before you send it out again. It would take you forever to query publishers. Get your query into the hands of as many publishers, editors, and readers as you possibly can. Don't expect to get a prompt response, because you won't. In fact, months can go by and you won't even be notified if your work has been received. It's important to keep a record of the date you sent your work and the name of the person it was sent to. You can also send your proposal certified mail. Allow six weeks to two months before you either write or call to inquire about the status of your work. I always prefer calling, because I know someone will take the time to give me an answer. At the very least, my call will be a reminder that I have sent my work to them. It's also an opportunity to try to establish a personal relationship with someone in the company, whether it's the receptionist or an editorial assistant. You can't afford to be passive in an arena where there are millions of people competing with you. By making follow-up calls, you're taking a positive action.

Before you start to send out your writing, find out what particular needs the publishers have and what types of manuscripts they're looking for. Do your homework first. You don't want to send your material to a publisher who isn't interested in your category of writing. Buy *Writer's Market*, published by Writer's Digest in Cincinnati. It's updated yearly and lists practically every magazine and book publisher. Study the books they publish to target your type of material to the right publisher. Or else you're wasting your time, energy, and money.

Study the trade papers so that you can learn which companies produce scripts like yours. Position yourself in the writing industry, so that you can realize your dreams and your writing goals. Be proactive and productive and keep your goal in sight at all times. Remember, "when the going gets tough, the tough get going."

When it comes to contracts, royalties, advances, and other business concerns, it's up to you to find out what you need to know to protect yourself. Make it your business to learn the business of writing.

Collaboration

You and your best friend are going to collaborate on a writing project. What could possibly go wrong? Well, a lot could go wrong, including your friendship.

To be prepared for the good fortune of having your script or manuscript optioned or sold, you need to have an agreement between you and your collaborator.

A collaboration is like a marriage. When it works, it's great. But as you know, 50 percent of marriages end in divorce. So protect yourself in advance, before you write the first word. With your cowriter, lay out a financial agreement, detail by detail. Write it down, sign it, have your cowriter sign it, and retain a copy. Forget handshakes or verbal promises. They just won't cut it, especially if you get a deal and your collaborator suddenly develops amnesia and forgets you helped write the script. I hear you saying to yourself, "Oh, this might happen with other people, but we're best friends." Don't you believe it. Better to be safe than sorry. Written agreements, even if on a sheet of notepaper, stand up in court better than verbal ones.

As for the writing itself, there are many methods to follow when you collaborate. Try them out and pick the one that best suits your personality and that of your writing partner. I've collaborated several times. In some of these partnerships, everything flowed, we were of like minds, and the writing went well. In others, the relationship was agonizing and the work drudgery.

Some collaborators write together, and others take different scenes of the script or novel. Then each reads what the other has written and revises or edits after it has been discussed. Before you write, you should agree that when a scene is especially important to either of you, that person will have the final say. Otherwise you'll be arguing about each and every word.

Put yourself in the other person's shoes and be sensitive to what she has written before you tear it apart. As in any good relationship, you need to show tact, respect, diplomacy, and sensitivity to the other person's feelings.

Believe it or not, some of the best writing I have done and the best times I have had, have been when I collaborated on several scripts. So keep what I said in mind and go for it.

Options

Options are the usual way of doing business in Hollywood. There are so many scripts circulating every day that production companies would go out of business if they had to put up a lot of option money to develop every script or manuscript they wanted to produce. Unfortunately for the writer, many companies want free options, and there are a great number of writers who give them just that. The usual amount of time is six months, and then it's renegotiated. In that time limit, the company will hopefully shop your project and make a deal.

Depending upon your status and your clout, you will either

agree to the terms or insist on a fee. There are pros and cons to giving away your project for free. If you are a new writer, you will probably be so excited that someone is interested in your project that you will agree to an option with no fee. And this might be a smart career move. It certainly is better to have someone circulating your project than to have it mildew in your closet.

I've given free options to individual producers who had contacts and track records but no money to put up for my project. In these cases, I had a concept or a proposal for a series, rather than a script.

On the other hand, I've also optioned a completed script with a major studio for thousands of dollars, only to have the studio fail to produce the script.

You must deal with each option agreement on an individual basis, with no rules written in concrete. Use common sense, set a limited period of time, and be certain that the company or individuals are excited about your project and will shop it around. Also, be sure any agreement is written and signed by both parties.

I discourage many writers from dealing with producers who want to option their completed script though they've never produced anything before. In these cases, it's wise to insist on money up front or find another producer who has credits.

Contracts

After your book proposal is accepted by a publisher, you will be sent a contract to sign. Remember, don't sign on the dotted line until you've read the contract.

Even if you're thrilled that your manuscript has been accepted, you need to protect yourself by having your agent read through and then negotiate the contract on your behalf.

Most publishers have developed the contract in their favor. After all, they are business people and would be foolish not to look out for themselves. Well, you, too, must be responsible for what you are willing to accept in the contract. An agent will study your contract, make deletions, and add clauses to protect your interests and your future sales.

Your contract will deal with how much of an advance you will receive and how many payments will be made. The contract will discuss your rights, your royalties, how many free copies you're entitled to, how the copyright will read, foreign distribution rights, and completion dates for the first draft, the rewrites, and the final draft.

Be sure you understand everything that's in the contract before you sign it, because once you sign, you are legally responsible—and that means you, not your lawyer or your agent. You should also set a deadline for the publication of your book. I think a year and a half is the most time you should give a publisher. Other people would allow two years. State in your contract that the book must be returned to you if it remains unpublished after the deadline has passed. Include a "reversion clause," which means the rights to the book revert back to you if the publisher stops publication.

After the final draft is submitted, it takes six to nine months for the book to be published.

The Advance

A writer usually gets an advance against royalties. The publisher pays an agreed-upon amount to the writer before the book is published and in some cases before it's even written. For a beginning writer, the advance is usually somewhere between three thousand and five thousand dollars. Many publishers break the advance into installments. For example, the payments might be made in three installments: when the contract is signed, when the manuscript is completed, and when the book is published. According to the Author's Guild, advances of five thousand dollars or less are received by 40 percent of all authors. The gigantic advances (six figures or more) are saved for a few best-selling writers or celebrities.

Royalties

A writer can't collect any of his royalties until the advance is paid off. Royalties are based on a sliding scale. Generally, the royalties for a hardcover book are 10 percent on the first five thousand copies, 12.5 percent on the next five thousand, and 15 percent thereafter. Paperback royalties range from 6 percent to 10 percent. The royalty rate for sales to book clubs is usually half as much as it is for sales to bookstores and individuals.

The Royalty Statement

Most royalty statements cover a six-month time frame, and they are usually very difficult to understand. The author often feels entitled to more money than the statement indicates. Don't hesitate to ask for an explanation of the statement. Most publishers keep back part of the royalty against returns. The amount that remains (if there is any) is the money owed you by the publisher.

After you have earned your advance, you should expect to start getting your royalties.

Subsidiary Rights

Retain your rights to your writing whenever possible. Know what your rights are before you sign them away. You should sell your rights for a limited period of time only and not forever. If a publisher doesn't publish your work, the rights should revert back to you after a certain period of time.

Be certain not to give your rights away when you sign a contract. What if a publisher goes bankrupt or is consolidated with another publisher and they decide not to publish your manuscript? If the rights don't revert back to you, you'll never be able to submit it to another publisher.

You also want to keep the rights to works for film, video, broadcast, and other electronic media. If you decide to sell these rights, you want to be very well-compensated.

Copyright

The copyright law passed in 1976 says the writer owns his or her work and a publisher is able to use the material only once unless special permission is provided in writing by the author.

Selling "first North American serial rights" to a manuscript might force you to give up some rights and will lock you in to the publisher buying it in the U.S. or Canada.

A good reference book about copyright is *Every Writer's Guide to Copyright and Publishing Law* by Ellen Kozak (Henry Holt).

When a writer completes his writing a copyright is in effect. The "new" copyright law took effect in 1978. It says that when a writer sells his work, he's selling *only* one-time rights. Your copyright protection lasts for the rest of your life and for fifty years after your death.

Your publisher usually will copyright in the author's name. Don't let a publisher copyright in the publisher's name only, because if you give up your copyright you give up all legal rights to your work and can't use the work again. Titles cannot be copyrighted.

All you need to do to protect your work is to display the copyright symbol © along with your name and date on the first page of your manuscript. To register your material with the U.S. Copyright Office, make out a check or money order to "Register of Copyrights," for the twenty-dollar registration fee and send it to the U.S. Copyright Office, Library of Congress, Washington,

D.C. 20559. Enclose one copy of the unpublished manuscript along with the completed application form.

Registering Your Script

You can protect your property from plagiarism by sending your unbound manuscript to the Writers Guild accompanied by a check for ten dollars if you're a member and twenty dollars if you're not, which will register your television or film script for five years. The title page must include your LEGAL name, return address, and Social Security number. Mail your manuscript to:

Writers Guild of America West
Registration Department
7000 West Third Street
Los Angeles, California 90048
(213) 782-4540

Kill Fees

A kill fee is given when a magazine assigns an article and then decides *not* to publish it. The kill fee ranges from 10 percent to 50 percent of the agreed-upon purchase price and varies with each magazine. It is your responsibility to find out what your publisher's standard kill fee is. You should have the terms regarding kill fees written into your contract.

As you conclude this chapter, I'm sure you now have a better direction of what you want to write, of the writing business, the writing markets and the world of contracts.

Keep reading and in the next chapter you will discover the "writer's world."

CHAPTER FOURTEEN

The Writer's World: From Writing Classes to Consultants

"Your vision is the promise of what you shall at last unveil."
—*John Ruskin*

Since 1980, when I taught my first writing class at UCLA there has been a tremendous increase in the number of classes offered to would-be writers, as well as a rising number of consultants, seminars, books, and tapes aimed at helping writers write.

Writing has become a big business. There is an entire world out there for writers that is getting more populated every day. This chapter is a guide to some of the many services offered to writers and how to find them.

Creative Writing Classes

You can take creative writing classes at the YMCA, through university extension programs, community colleges, and adult education programs at local high schools.

The following schools have adult education classes in writing and scriptwriting:

UCLA Extension, Writers' Program
10995 LeConte Avenue
Los Angeles, California 90024

American Film Institute, Public Programs
2021 North Western Avenue
Los Angeles, California 90027

For more information on creative writing courses, write to:

Associated Writing Programs
c/o Old Dominion University
Norfolk, Virginia 23529

Writer's Clubs

The California Writer's Club has various regional memberships. There are monthly meetings where members hear guest speakers and exchange information on writing contests and other outlets for their work. They also put out a newsletter.

Sisters in Crime is a group for women mystery writers. Romance Writers of America has regional clubs throughout the United States.

If you attend writing classes in your area, make a list of the students in your class who have writing goals similar to yours and form your own writing group after the class is finished. The advantage to forming groups from a writing workshop is that you already know each other's writing project, you've formed relationships and have a similar approach to your craft, based on what you were taught in the workshop. Many of my former students have formed personal relationships, others formed writing groups with a set meeting time and place to discuss their work on a weekly or monthly basis. Others have successfully collaborated with each other, eventually selling their scripts and novels.

If you haven't taken a formal class and want to get feedback for your writing, get together with acquaintances or friends who will share the same enthusiasm for writing as you. It's important to have ground rules for your group, because if you don't, it's just too easy to socialize and not discuss the work at hand. You should take your group and it's rules seriously. Anyone who doesn't comply or respect the rules shouldn't be in the group.

Groups differ in their approaches to the writing. Some allot an entire evening to the reading of just one work. Others give everyone a chance to discuss their works-in-progress, reading as little as a couple of pages a night. In any case, it's important to establish what's comfortable for the group. However, there are certain rules that are imperative:

1. Give everyone a copy of the work to be read. It is much easier to critique writing that you can see as well as hear.

2. Allow no destructive criticism. Anyone who wants to make a comment has to make it constructive—saying what doesn't work and giving suggestions on how to make it work.

3. Make no judgments on *content*. If someone is writing a novel about an abortion, your stand on the abortion issue should *not* be the focus of a critique. Any discussion should be about the writing itself, and whether it has a well-constructed plot, for instance, and interesting characters.

4. Stick to a schedule, so that one participant doesn't get only ten minutes of feedback, because the first writer got two hours.

5. Make a commitment to yourself and to the rest of the group to show up. If you don't attend a meeting because you haven't written anything, you're letting yourself down, as well as the rest of the group. You'll discover that it's easier to hear criticism that applies to your own writing when it's aimed at others. Somehow you aren't as defensive or close-minded when someone else's work is being critiqued. You'll be surprised at how many ideas you'll get for yourself from listening to people discuss another writer's work.

Correspondence Courses in Writing

Correspondence courses for writers are advertised in *Writer's Digest* or *The Writer* magazines. The requirements for these courses differ with each school. Usually you'll receive assignments that must be turned in at a specific time. You should receive critiques of your writing. Usually these will be made by a teacher or mentor assigned to you. Find out all the information you can about a school and its staff before you send your money.

Writing Conferences

Writer's conferences bring you together with editors, authors, agents, and publishers. A beginning or experienced writer can make contacts and network with other writers.

If you want a complete listing of all the conferences available to writers, you can purchase *The Guide to Writers Conferences,* published by Shawguides.

When you attend a workshop or conference, it is certainly appropriate to introduce yourself to any agent or editor who you think would be right for your work. Tell them about your project, with enthusiasm and focus. Ask if you may send your query letter, proposal, or manuscript to them. The worst thing they can do is say no, and in that case, you're no farther behind than you were.

When you send your writing to the contact you made at the conference, include a cover letter and refer to your conversation. That may jolt their memory enough to put a face to the name on your work. It's to your advantage to make as many contacts as you can at these conferences. I believe it's almost more important than the workshops. (I am assuming, of course, that you have polished your writing and that it is professional, well-crafted, and ready to be sent out.)

The following is a partial list of writing conferences throughout the United States and Canada:

Iowa Summer Writing Festival
Iowa City, Iowa (May through July)

Haystack Writing Program
Cannon Beach, Oregon (July and August)

Society of Children's Book Writers
National Conference
Los Angeles, California (August)

Aspen Writers' Conference
Aspen, Colorado (July)

The Maui Writers Conference
Maui, Hawaii (August)

Stonecoast Writers' Conference
Freeport, Maine (July)

Napa Valley Writers' Conference
Napa, California (July)

Bennington Summer Writing Workshops
Bennington, Vermont (June and July)

Bread Loaf Writers Conference
Ripton, Vermont (August)

Sewanee Writers' Conference
The University of the South
Sewanee, Tennesee (July)

Port Townsend Writers Conference
Centrum Foundation
Port Townsend, Washington (July)

The Cape Cod Writers' Center
Barnstable, Massachusetts (August)

Fine Arts Work Center Summer Workshops
Provincetown, Massachusetts (June through August)

Bluegrass Writers' Workshop
Lousiville, Kentucky (June)

Jackson Hole Writer's Conference
Jackson Hole, Wyoming (Late June)

Writer's Colonies

Writer's colonies provide a retreat for writers where they can work without interruption, often in an effort to finish a work-in-progress. Requirements and costs vary. Some colonies offer meals, and some don't. I've worked with many individuals who were able to complete their writing projects while staying at a writer's colony. They had quiet, solitude, and lots of time to work, and some colonies offered daily discussion of the work-in-progress.

For more information on writers' colonies, write to:

Center of Arts Information
1285 Avenue of the Americas
New York, New York 10019

Writer's workshops and conferences are listed in certain issues of the following publication, usually in the spring:

Writer's Digest
1507 Dana Avenue
Cincinnati, Ohio 45207

An additional list of grants and awards available to American writers is published by:

Pen American Center
568 Broadway
New York, New York 10012

The following is a partial list of Writers' Colonies:

Blue Mountain Center
Blue Mountain Lake
New York, New York 12812

Cottages at Hedgebrook
2197 East Millman Road
Langley, Washington 98260
(360) 321-4786

The Macdowell Colony
100 High Street
Peterborough, New Hampshire 03458
(603) 924-3886

Oregon Writers Colony House
P.O. Box 15200
Portland, Oregon 97293
(503) 827-8072

Ragdale Foundation
1260 North Green Bay Road
Lake Forest, Illinois 60045
(847) 234-1063

Virginia Center for the Creative Arts
Box VCCA
Sweet Briar, Virginia 24595
(804) 946-7236

Yaddo
P.O. Box 395
Saratoga Springs, New York 12866

Script Consultants

"Admitting a problem is halfway to a solution."

—*Anonymous*

Say you've spent weeks, months, or years on your novel, script, or short story, and it's just not working. What better way to solve the problem than by getting help from a consultant? If you think about the potential money you can make with a best-selling novel or a blockbuster script, doesn't it make sense to have your writing be devoid of any flaws or problems?

I have consulted with hundreds of people who were ready to send their script or manuscript out in deplorable condition. One person had a 300-page script, another had an 87-page script, neither one of which was the proper length for a screenplay. Let me tell you now that nobody would read either of those scripts.

A script consultant will ask the following types of questions: Does your story have a proper structure? Does it have a beginning, a middle, and an end? Does your main character have a goal that drives the plot? Are your characters motivated and consistent in personality and behavior? Is your story interesting? Does it fall apart in the middle?

I have been surprised by the poor storytelling and character development of many works by professional writers. They have sent me their scripts and manuscripts for consultation without a story, with no character goals, and with uninteresting characters who were either inconsistent or one-dimensional.

The Ten Most Common Mistakes Writers Make

1. No clear-cut main character.

2. No *specific*, desperate goal for the main character.

3. No spine or story structure.

4. Chapters or scenes that have no connection to one another.

5. All the characters sound the same.

6. The dialogue is conversational and doesn't further the plot.

7. The character's behavior is *not* motivated.

8. The writing is episodic, with no underlying plot holding it together.

9. The book or script has no overall purpose.

10. The author doesn't have any idea what he or she wants to say through the characters.

When should you turn to a consultant for help? When your structure doesn't work. When your main character is weak and boring. When your story isn't working. When you develop writer's block. When you aren't sure if this is the best writing you can do.

When you send your script or manuscript to editors, producers, publishers, or agents, you want it to represent the best writing you're capable of. As I stated before, you don't have a second chance to make a first impression. Neither does your script. What better way to ensure this is your best effort than by consulting with a professional?

Don't give your writing to your lover, sister, mother, father, friend, or enemy to critique. You're just asking for trouble, and you might sabotage a good relationship. Go to a professional writing consultant if you want professional feedback (and hang on to your friends and family).

The following is a list of just a few script consultants who have good track records. For further information, read the writing magazines like *Writer's Digest* and *The Writer,* where you'll find many consultants who advertise.

Linda Seger
2038 Louella Avenue
Venice, California 90291
(310) 390-1951

Linda Seger is a well-known script doctor and lecturer and the author of four books: *Making a Good Script Great, Creating Unforgettable Characters, The Art of Adaptation: Turning Fact and Fiction into Film,* and *From Script to Screen: The Collaborative Art of Filmmaking.* She conducts seminars nationally and internationally. Her fifth book is *When Women Call the Shots.*

Lisa Alexander
Scriptcraft
955 Galloway Street
Pacific Palisades,California 90272
(310) 454-6954

Lisa Alexander is a script consultant.

Michael Hauge
Hilltop Productions
P.O. Box 55728
Sherman Oaks, California 91013
(818) 995-4209

Michael Hauge is a script consultant who conducts seminars nationwide. He is the author of *Writing Screenplays That Sell.*

Christopher Vogler
941 Amoroso Place
Venice, California 90291
(310) 822-1587

Chris Vogler is the author of *The Writer's Journey: Mythic Structure for Storyteller and Screenwriters* and lectures on mythic story structure. He is also a story analyst.

David Trottier
The Screenwriting Center
869 East 4500 South, Suite 10
Salt Lake City, Utah 84107-3049

David Trottier is the author of *The Screenwriter's Bible.* He does script analysis, conducts seminars, and offers correspondence courses.

Rachel Ballon's
Writer's Center
P.O. Box 491414
Los Angeles, California 90049
(310) 479-0048

Ballon is the author of *Blueprint for Writing,* founder and director of the Writer's Center, a writer's consultant, teacher, and psychotherapist. She specializes in writer's issues such as procrastination, writer's block, and story structure. She provides script and book consultations, and phone sessions with writers. She also conducts workshops and seminars nationally and internationally.

Agents

Never, never, never pay an agent to read your material. Some agents or would-be agents make a living by charging reading fees and do nothing else! These agents can make a healthy income by just charging reading fees for submissions and never selling a manuscript or making a legitimate deal.

If you are a screen or television writer, for a nominal fee you can get a list of agents from the Writer's Guild of America, 7000 West Third Street, Los Angeles, California 90048; (213) 951-4000.

For those of you writing fiction and nonfiction, *Publisher's Weekly* is a good reference for finding new literary agencies and available markets. Another resource for book writers is the *Insider's Guide to Book Editors, Publishers, and Literary Agents,* by Jeff Herman. Copies may be ordered from Prima Publishing, P.O. Box 1260BK, Rocklin, California 95677; (916) 632-4400.

How to Get an Agent

It's always better to have a referral before you call an agent. If you can get a referral from someone the agent knows, at least you can say, "Mark Smith suggested that I call you." This puts you a step ahead of the cold caller. Agents will usually be receptive if you have the name of one or more of their clients.

If you don't have a personal referral, try to find one. Go to writers' organizations, workshops, conferences, and classes, and don't just sit there—network. Make friends, make contacts, make connections—if not for your present work, then for future projects.

If that doesn't work, be creative. Get a list of agents and find out who some of their clients are, then call the agent and say you're an avid fan of Mrs. ABC, or that your writing is similar to Mr. XYZ's. Obviously, this isn't the best solution, but it's a start.

Do your research: Find out who each agent represents and what types of books he or she is looking for before querying or calling. Don't call a literary agent who specializes in historical novels if your book is a mystery. Or don't send your high-tech, action-adventure showcase script to an agent who represents sitcom writers.

After you sign the contract, an agent works for you and is *your* employee. Does this sound strange? You probably can't even think in those terms, for in reality, any writer is thrilled to get an agent. It all goes back to the law of supply and demand, and in this business, the demand for agents far exceeds the supply.

I often consult with writers who have an agent but don't know how to relate to them. In most cases, they are afraid to call their agents because they don't want to make him or her angry or seem like a pest. Many of them are upset because their agents never return their phone calls.

As grateful as you are after you get your agent, remember that he or she *works for you.* The agent makes money from the sale of your book or screenplay and gets a percentage of your profits. With that in mind, let me share some of the strategies I have suggested to these writers for dealing with their agents.

First, I helped them work out a specific plan that hinged on their taking an active role in their career. I had them reframe their attitude, so that rather than sitting back and waiting for something to happen, or calling with an I-hope-I'm-not-bothering-you attitude, they learned to call with specific information to help their agent.

For example, they might say, "I ran into the producer Sue Roberts at Spagos, and she'd like you to send my script to her at Paramount."

This change of attitude made them sound confident and capable. It helped them form a better, more equal relationship with their agent.

As you begin to take charge of your career, you'll feel more empowered, and your agent will have more respect for you.

Most agents on the West Coast submit to studios or networks. If a New York agent is representing your book or article, he or she will probably work in conjunction with a West Coast agent, and they will split the commission. Agents who represent television and film writers are regulated by the Writers Guild of America. Guild rules determine the commission they may charge, which is 10 percent.

Literary agents, however, can ask for 15 to 20 percent or even more. They aren't under the jurisdiction of the Writers Guild of America.

Developing a Good Relationship with Your Agent

A successful Hollywood literary agent spoke to a writing group at my Writer's Center. The following are some of the tips she gave the writers after they got an agent:

1. Be productive.

2. Network—meet people in the business.

3. Keep writing new material.

4. Be aggressive.

5. Look for opportunities.

6. Take action.

7. Be friendly.

8. Never give up.

Who is your writing career more important to—the agent or you? The answer is obvious. That's why you need to do everything you can to motivate your agent to work for you. After all, you're just one person in a stable of many writers. Actively participate in your own career and call your agent with leads and suggestions that may help make a sale.

This is not to say there isn't a fine line between staying on top of your writing projects and becoming a nuisance. The last thing you want to do is antagonize your agent and the staff.

What Type of Agent Do You Want?

Do you only want to be with a big agency like CAA, ICM, or William Morris, where you might be a little fish in the big pond? Or would you feel more comfortable in a smaller agency, where your agent might be less powerful than one at a big agency but will probably work harder for you.

My advice is to do what makes you feel comfortable. What's important is that you develop a good working relationship with your agent based on mutual respect. This is especially important if you are a new writer and need to get that first script sold.

Don't be intimidated by your agent. If your phone calls constantly remain unanswered and unreturned, it's up to you to discuss this with him. If he is arrogant and unresponsive, it might be better to look for a new agent, rather than continually suffering from fear and frustration.

Literary or Entertainment Lawyers

Many successful writers have never had an agent but prefer to use entertainment or literary attorneys to negotiate their contracts.

Since writers who don't have agents usually don't get as good a deal as they would have received if they had one, it's important to protect yourself if you don't have an agent. When a publisher or production company wants to do a deal with you, it would benefit you to hire a lawyer to either read through the contract and advise you or to negotiate the deal on your behalf. The language of a contract is very legalistic, and you probably won't understand what it is you're reading.

If you hire an attorney, ask for an hourly rate and decide whether it's worth the cost up front. To protect yourself and your product, it seems to me a reasonable and intelligent investment to hire a lawyer. After you pay the lawyer's fee, you're finished paying, whereas an agent gets a commission on your work forever.

On the other hand, you don't pay in advance with an agent. You only pay when you start getting royalties.

I have twice used an attorney to negotiate a contract for me when I sold a work without the help of an agent. Why would I share my royalties with an agent, I reasoned, after I had made the deal myself? Yet, I still needed to have someone represent me who was knowledgeable about literary contracts. Using each of these attorneys was profitable in the long run. They were my advocates and looked out for my best interests. Susan Schaeffer, the attorney who drew up an option agreement for me with a major Hollywood Studio, protected my rights both present and future. And when I made a deal with a publisher who wanted to buy *Blueprint for Writing*, I didn't need an agent. I was represented by Steve Fayne, an experienced entertainment and literary attorney. Steve negotiated the book contract for me and protected my rights down the line.

If you want to find an attorney to negotiate your contract or to give you legal advice pertaining to publishing or producing, you can call the bar association in your area and get a list of attorneys who specialize in representing writers.

The Query Letter

Whether you use an agent or attempt to get your book or screenplay published yourself, you need to know how to write a query letter and a book proposal. Agents and editors don't have the time or inclination to read an entire unsolicited manuscript until they are excited by your query letter or book proposal. Never send a manuscript without first sending a query letter. If you do, it will be returned without comment.

It is of the utmost importance to write a dynamite query letter. It should be no longer than one typewritten page, although there are exceptions to this rule. Recently, a client of mine sent a three-page query that included a synopsis of his novel. It was so interesting that four agents called wanting to represent him. (See Appendix B.)

Publishers and editors are sent thousands of letters, proposals, and manuscripts each month and don't have the time to read all of them. Can you imagine how much it would cost them to send back each submission if you didn't enclose a self-addressed, stamped envelope? So without an SASE, you won't get a response. It's your responsibility to enclose one (*with the correct postage*) if you want your manuscript back. And that means including an envelope large enough to hold your manuscript! To make certain your proposal or submission has arrived at its destination, send it by certified mail, return receipt requested.

When you type a query letter, use good bond paper. Put your name in the upper left-hand corner and the page number in the upper right-hand corner, followed by a key word from your title.

For example:

Rachel Ballon   #3.   BLUEPRINT

Don't eliminate yourself from the competition by sending a
sloppy query letter. You must proofread everything you write
before you send it out, even if you're using a spelling check,
which doesn't catch words that are properly spelled but incor-
rectly used. Send a neat, clean, properly typed manuscript, using
the correct margins, spelling, punctuation, and grammar. Your
query letter should represent your writing at its best. It's disap-
pointing enough to have your query meet with rejection, as 98
percent of all queries do, so don't add to the chances by sending
a mediocre letter.

When you write a query letter, don't brag about what a fabulous writer you are. And don't brag about your idea being the
greatest in all the world." This is a real turn off. Publishers and
editors know what is good and what isn't, and they have a defi-
nite idea of what kind of material they want to publish. They
don't have to be told by you.

Sometimes it helps to identify the potential market for your
work. Is it targeted to the aging baby boomers or to teenagers?
And is the potential market one that the publisher you're con-
tacting is interested in?

The last part of your query letter should list your qualifica-
tions as a writer on this particular subject. Talk about your experience in the field and include anything that adds to your
credibility. If you have any material supporting your claims of
expertise, include it. Do anything possible to build up your credibility and visibility. Convince the publisher that you are the person best qualified for the job.

If your query letter is well-written and you support all your
claims, the rest is all based on the needs and wants of the publisher.
A rejection doesn't mean your work isn't any good. It just means
"We're not buying what you're selling." That's it. Nothing more.

If you're proud of your proposal, put the rejection slip in a file folder and get on with the next submission.

Your query letter is your selling tool. Hopefully, it will give the buyer confidence that you can deliver what you promised. And that's why you have to be specific. Target your proposal, and give the buyer what he needs to help him say yes to your query.

Wait between four to six weeks, and then follow up with a phone call. Was your letter received? If yes, what is the status of your material?

Most editors discourage writers from calling before sending a query. However, I've had some luck doing just that. By calling, I established a rapport with someone in the company before sending my query. I also was able to find out if that particular publisher or agent was interested in the type of writing I was doing.

There is no iron-clad rule. If you decide to call before you send a query letter, relate your idea in a couple of short sentences. Have enthusiasm and sound confident and knowledgeable. You are the expert in your particular subject. Be prepared to answer any questions asked by the editor or publisher.

There is an outside chance that your idea could be stolen by a staff writer. I recall pitching an idea to an entertainment magazine over the phone and getting a rejection, only to be called a few months later by a staff writer who asked to interview me for the very same article.

What do you think I did after I got over the shock? I gave her an interview. There was no way I could prove it was my idea, so I decided to benefit from being referred to in the article as an expert.

On the other hand, you could establish a relationship via the telephone and create interest for your project that you couldn't convey in a letter. You want to stress that your idea is timely, of interest to the publication's readership, and universal in appeal.

Read everything you can about your field so that your writing will be fresh and original. Become an expert. Don't rewrite what's already been written, but bring a new approach to an old subject. Reinvent the wheel.

The Manuscript

When a manuscript is sent without being requested it is known as an unsolicited manuscript. Unsolicited manuscripts are also said to come in "over the transom." It is never wise to submit an entire manuscript without first sending a proposal or query letter. If you do, it will end up in the "slush pile"—the pile of unsolicited manuscripts, most of which are never read. (There are always exceptions, of course. In fact, some wonderful books have been discovered this way.)

When you send an article proposal to a magazine, you can also submit a tear sheet of your published work, which demonstrates your writing style. Newspaper articles are referred to as "clips."

Manuscripts should be typed on 8½-by-11-inch white bond paper, double-spaced, with margins between 1 and 1½ inches. Do not use a justified right-hand margin, since it often results in loose spacing between words.

All manuscripts must be typed. If you don't type, hire a professional typist. You can probably find several listed in the Yellow Pages of your phone book or in the classified ads of your local newspaper. Typists and word processors also advertise in the back of most writing magazines.

Always keep the original of your writing and send a copy. If you have used a computer, don't include a disk with the manuscript unless the publisher requests it.

On the first page of your manuscript, include your name, address, city, state, zip code, and telephone number in the upper left-hand corner. Your book title and your name should be centered and double-spaced above the beginning of your text, starting halfway down the page. In the upper right-hand corner, you can include the approximate word count. (There are approximately 250 words to a page.)

Always use first-class mail when you submit articles, query letters, proposals, and writing samples. Manuscripts for your fiction or nonfiction books may be sent fourth class or book rate, but they'll take longer to reach their destination. It seems to me to be well worth the extra cost to send your precious manuscript first class. To make certain your proposal or submission has arrived, send it by certified mail, return receipt requested.

The Book Proposal

After you have the correct margins, spelling, and grammar, you need to be certain the content of your proposal is clear, exciting, concise, and interesting enough to grab the executive, editor, or publisher who reads it. (See Appendix C.)

Creating an exciting book proposal is not an easy task. It takes time, energy, motivation, and a lot of hard work. You must rework your proposal until it's perfect. After all, this is your advertisement for the product you will deliver. Since you can't take out an ad in the *Wall St. Journal* telling everyone how many benefits they'll receive by giving you an advance or contract, you'll have to sell them through your proposal. And you only have one shot to do it. Here are some tips that will help you.

1. Have a well-thought-out chapter outline for your entire book. In one to three paragraphs, state the essence of each chapter, using strong prose and clear writing. Be sure to include a table of contents, to give an immediate idea of what the entire book is about.

2. Include from one to three sample chapters. These chapters should represent your writing at its best. Be sure your transitions are natural and the writing flows from one chapter to another. Show how well-organized your ideas are and that you're able to put together a cohesive book.

3. You need to include who you are, either with a résumé or a profile. If you're writing a nonfiction book, include your credentials and such supporting materials as a list of classes you've taught, articles you've published, and promotional materials. These will give you added credibility in your field.

4. Target the audience for your book, after having done the necessary research by going to bookstores and seeing what the competition is in your particular genre. How is your book different from the rest? What makes it fresh and original? (This is where your salesmanship comes in. Go for it with facts, not fluff.) Don't tell them what a fabulous person you are, even if it's so. Just state the facts and no hyperbole, please.

Synopsis

Some publishers want a synopsis of your book, telling the story from beginning to end. Writing a powerful synopsis that will intrigue the reader is an art in itself. Your synopsis can range from three pages to thirty. However, telling your story in fewer pages and compressing the action is more exciting. The average synopsis is one to five pages.

Here are some helpful hints to make your synopsis exciting:

1. Tell your story in present-tense prose, and use strong visual images.

2. Use concrete words and active verbs. Forget the passive voice.

3. Avoid dialogue.

4. Eliminate unessential details, but set the major event of the story on stage, scene by scene.

5. Write your synopsis through your main character's point of view.

6. If you have many characters, include a cast of characters, with a brief description of each, in the beginning.

Your writing tools are your selling tools. They are your calling cards. Make them buyer-friendly!

CHAPTER FIFTEEN

Breaking Through the Barriers: From Writing Blocks to Writing Blockbusters

"Life is either a daring adventure or nothing."

— *Helen Keller*

I looked up the words *persistent* and *consistent* in my thesaurus and found the following words: *steady, tenacious, constant, unwavering, continuous, persevering, unflagging, tireless, unrelenting.* These qualities are what it takes to be a successful writer. Without being consistent in your writing and persistent in trying to sell and market it, you will not succeed. Over and over again, I've seen some of the most talented writing students fail to make it because they gave up in frustration somewhere in their writing journey.

In the fable of the tortoise and the hare, these two unequal opponents raced together and everyone laughed at the turtle, but he just kept on moving toward his destination and focused on his goal. Slow and steady, unrelenting and unwavering. And against all odds, he won the race. In the same way, you can master your craft and overcome obstacles to your writing if you persist.

On the other hand, if you are talented and writing comes easily to you, if you can string words together to form beautiful images but don't persist with your writing, you won't reach your goal. Good writing takes repetition and practice, just like any skill. So have perseverance and diligence and approach your writing as you would any challenge you wish to meet. Write every day, even if it's only for fifteen to thirty minutes. Have the courage to fight for your work when it's not happening. Be resilient and flexible and don't give up.

Criticism

> "People ask you for criticism, but they only want praise."
>
> —W. Somerset Maugham

When I began attending writing workshops years ago, I was so insecure about my craft that I'd be devastated by criticism. I attended many writing workshops and had a multitude of experiences in them. Some teachers were wonderful and nurturing; others were rigid and dogmatic.

At some point, I discovered that in order to develop my own style, I had to listen to my inner voices and let them sing across the page.

This is the advice I give my students: Listen to and trust your own voice, and write about your passion.

When you take writing workshops, or classes or when a friend gives you feedback on your latest script, novel, or short story, remember that all criticism is subjective. If your writing style is like Hemingway's and I like Melville's works, my judgment of your work will be influenced by the differences in our tastes.

Assuming you have mastered your craft and the rudiments of writing, criticism then gets into personal preferences, judgments, and opinions. Each teacher will have his or her favorite writers and authors.

Constructive criticism is fine, especially when someone makes a suggestion targeted to a specific writing problem. That is the only type of criticism I ever permit in my classes. It's important not to let any teacher, colleague, or friend be destructive in their criticism of your work. Don't ever allow anyone to say, "You're writing stinks," or "That isn't any good."

If you get that kind of feedback from a teacher or another student, run, don't walk, to the nearest exit. And on the way, ask for your money back.

A good teacher will look at the writing to see if the characters are multifaceted and multidimensional; if the story is motivated and well-structured; and if the dialogue is clear and crisp and moves the story along.

So don't get depressed if you feel you've done the best you can do and your writing style just doesn't happen to be what the teacher, editor, or producer likes. Now, the important words in that sentence are *if you feel you've done the best you can do*. In other words, you ultimately have to judge your writing for yourself and believe in your own ability.

On the other hand, if everyone who reads your work has the same criticism—e.g., "The main character isn't active"; "the script falls apart in the second act"; "your dialogue is too conversational and doesn't have enough conflict"—then you need to look at what you've written and be willing to make the necessary changes. Wouldn't you want to do this anyway, until you produced the best piece of writing you're capable of producing?

If you don't know what to do to make your script work, consult a script doctor or writing consultant. You must be flexible enough to make changes in your script, book, or play when they're warranted. Don't let your pride overcome your better judgment.

This will only happen if you are confident in your ability as a writer. If you're insecure, asking everyone for his or her opinion and making countless changes according to what they suggest, then your original reason for writing will get lost in the chaos of criticism and contradictory opinions. You'll then have nothing of yourself left in your writing.

When people give me their script for consultation and I critique their work, I always make a point of saying, "This is just my opinion, and ultimately, you must decide what *you* want to do with my suggestions, because it's your writing."

If any writing instructor insists that his way is the only way, listen to what he says and then do what you want to do. Of course, if you're taking the course for credit, this may not be prudent. Perhaps you can give the instructor what he wants and then, when you're ready to write your story to sell, write it the way *you* want.

Don't let anyone's criticism stifle your creativity and your spirit. Criticism is only someone's personal opinion, and the only opinion that ultimately counts is yours. Your goal is to have your writing be the best possible representation of your talent and ability when you send it out. Your writing is you. Show your best to the world.

Rejection

"To try and fail is at least to learn. To fail to try is to suffer the inestimable loss of what might have been."

—*Chester Barnard*

Whenever you receive a rejection letter, don't take it personally. It's just that the buyer isn't buying what you're selling. Make this an opportunity to begin a relationship with the publisher by sending a personal note saying you appreciate the consideration your manuscript received. If the rejection is more than a form letter, write and thank the sender for his sage advice, adding that you are going to employ it in the rewriting of your manuscript. Failure is not being rejected. Failure is giving up. So believe in yourself and trust what you've written. Who's to say that your next submission won't be the one that's bought?

Always have something you've written in the marketplace. Whether it's a query letter, a manuscript, a script, or a poem, keep sending it out. I had a poetry teacher who told me that instead of getting depressed when I received a rejection, I should get another copy of my poetry into the mail immediately. So be like a juggler and have many manuscripts making the rounds. Overcome rejection by rejecting it.

Writer's Block

"The smallest action is better than the largest plan."

—*John Groves*

Many writers become blocked when their work gets rejected—whether it's the first time or the fiftieth. Others become blocked when they begin writing a new scene or chapter. One good way to get unblocked is to stop your writing session before you finish the scene you're working on. Then, the next time you sit down to write, it will be easier to get started than it would be if you had to worry about beginning a new scene. You'll know exactly where you're going and how to get there.

You can also try retyping or rewriting a couple of pages you already have written, to get the rhythm of your words. With luck, your writing will just flow into the next scene.

If you get blocked when facing the empty page, lightly put marks on the page with a pencil, so it won't intimidate you by being blank. Another idea is to read your favorite poetry for ten to fifteen minutes before you start to write. This gets your mind into the meter and rhythm of the poem. It also relaxes you and quiets your self-doubts and fears.

These are just a few basic techniques for overcoming writer's block. But writer's block can be a very complex phenomenon, and sometimes it's not that easy to break through.

When I consult with writers who are blocked, I first try to find out what's going on in their life, to determine whether the problem is with the writing or with the writer. In talking to them,

I often discover the block is connected to what's going on in their life at the moment and has nothing to do with the writing.

There are so many reasons for writer's block that a simple solution to the cause isn't possible. Most of you will find yourself blocked at some time during your writing career. Often writer's block comes from thoughtless or insensitive criticisms in classes or by family members. The best way to avoid this type of block, is to avoid showing your writing to your mother, father, lover, brother, neighbor, or coworker, until it's finished and you're satisfied with it. If you show your work too soon in the writing process, you're allowing yourself to be vulnerable to other people's opinions and criticisms. That is a sure-fire way to become blocked.

Blocks frequently stem from personal difficulties. If you've just been fired or are going through a divorce, a death, or a disappointment, these will affect your writing. Economic insecurity, family dysfunctions, and relationship problems often cause writer's block.

Many blocks originate from an unconscious need for self-protection. Sometimes writers can't write because they fear failure.

How can you be rejected if you don't write? How can you be disappointed if you're not criticized? How can you fail if you can't work?

Blocks are often caused by internal forces such as insecurity, fear of failure, fear of success, fear of rejection, negative self-talk, unrealistic expectations, procrastination, depression, and repressed emotions.

But what if you desperately want to write more than anything in the world? You sit at your computer day after day and you can't write. Feelings of frustration, depression, and sadness come over you. You don't know where to start. You don't know what to write. You don't know how to overcome the block. You lose your confidence in yourself and in your writing. You sit at your desk and aren't able to produce any words on the empty page. Every day you go to your computer or your typewriter to write and the well is dry. *What do you do? How do you overcome this block?*

Well, the first thing you do is identify the block. You can't fight a problem if you don't know what the problem is. To this end, I have identified the following six stumbling blocks that often prevent writers from writing. All of these blocks are really different aspects of fear. Try to discover which one is causing your block.

Six Stumbling Blocks to Writing

1. Procrastination

2. Fear of success or failure

3. Fear of rejection

4. Psychological and creative blocks

5. Inner critic

6. Negative frame of mind

These blocks cause most of the problems writers experience when they sit down to write and become immobilized. They are responsible for preventing you from getting started on a project or from finishing it or getting it into the marketplace. They keep you stuck in the middle of your work, creating resistance to writing itself and diminishing your belief in your talent and ability. They can lead to low self-esteem and insecurity. They decrease your creativity and productivity while increasing your stress.

How does each block affect you? Can you identify the one that causes you the most frustration and pain. Take your time in looking over the list, and when you're ready, take a pen and paper and write about the block that causes you the most trouble. Write as fast as you can for twenty minutes, without rereading your work or editing it. Just keep your hand moving on the page until you're finished. Now read over what you've written. Are there any surprises? Do you have a better insight into your writer's block?

> "Defeat is a school in which truth always grows stronger."
>
> —*Harriet Ward Beecher*

By identifying your block and getting in touch with the real cause, you will be able to overcome it. Remember, you can't overcome a problem if you aren't aware of it.

On a conscious level, sometimes writers aren't willing to put in the hard work and the discipline to overcome their blocks. So if you completed the exercise and still feel blocked—*just write anyway.* If you don't write, you'll never break through your block. So take the action of writing, and remember that it doesn't have to be right—just write it! The process of writing will eventually help you overcome your block.

Procrastination

> "Putting off an easy thing makes it difficult."
>
> —*George H. Lormier*

One of the most common reactions to writer's block is to procrastinate. What better way not to get rejected than just not to finish your writing! I've consulted with many writers who feel ashamed, guilty, and frustrated because they don't ever get started, or having started, they don't finish their writing project. They procrastinate by doing other things, such as going shopping, sharpening pencils, cooking, cleaning the house, mowing the lawn, or shoveling snow.

Procrastination is insidious and pervasive. The only way to fight it is by writing. Write and you will no longer procrastinate. If this remedy sounds easy, it isn't. But what choice do you have? If you act against your feelings and just keep writing, you'll eventually overcome your block. It doesn't really matter why you procrastinate. You can spend, days, weeks, months, or years just looking for the reason, and when you finally discover it, what do you do then? You write. So fight it and just write no matter what.

Another reason people procrastinate is that when the writing becomes difficult, they look for ways to avoid it. They get involved in an activity that provides them with immediate gratification, such as eating, drinking, going to movies, talking on the phone, or watching television. These activities take no discipline or concentration. If the writer persists in these forms of entertainment and escape, he won't have time to write and will never overcome his writer's block.

One of the best ways to break through your writer's block is to act against your fears. Don't think about writing or worry about it or feel guilty about it—just *do it*. You'll find that all the time and energy you wasted in worrying about your block will now be used instead in the act of writing. When you overcome your block, you'll feel a new sense of freedom when you write. Breaking free of blocks is an exhilarating and personally rewarding experience. Keep writing and hopefully you'll go from blocks to best-sellers and blockbusters.

The following are ten keys to help you overcome your blocks:

Ten Keys to Overcoming Writer's Block

1. Stay in the moment.

2. Suspend critical judgments.

3. Be open to all possibilities.

4. Forget about results.

5. Silence your inner critic.

6. Be in the process and not the product.

7. Embrace your playful child.

8. Lose your ego.

9. Be courageous.

10. Reveal yourself.

Overcoming writer's block frees up your creative imagination and allows you to make your writing a joyful experience filled with creative energy, spirit, and imagination.

Revisions and Rewriting

> "The gem cannot be polished without friction, nor man perfected without trials."
>
> — Confucius

There are those rare occasions when writing takes a short time. But most of the time, writing is *rewriting*. Sometimes you'll do four, five, or more drafts until it works. Don't shortchange yourself by accepting your first draft if it doesn't reflect your best writing. Through rewriting and rewriting and rewriting, you'll develop the techniques you need to make your work professional.

As you keep writing, you add layers to your characters, giving them a heart and soul and breathing life into your story, applying twists and turns. It takes confidence and courage to continue to write until you've given it your best effort.

When you rewrite, you want to adhere to the saying "Less is more." This means you want to get rid of excess adverbs, adjectives, explanations, and redundancies. You want to trim and cut so that your writing is tight, clear, and concise. When you're finished with your rewrites and revisions, read over your writing as if you had never seen it before. Does it have a focus? Is the focus clear? Do you use active verbs? Do you constantly repeat yourself and explain what you want to write rather than just writing it?

Rewriting is probably the most important aspect of the writing process. When you rewrite, you need to keep cutting and clearing away the weeds of confusion. Clean up your dangling participles and trim your excess verbiage. As you revise, try to express your thoughts on the page in the most exciting way possible. To rewrite is to communicate and connect with your readers.

Think of obstacles to writing as challenges or opportunities. Writing is a wonderful gift. It allows you to be creative and to express your thoughts, your ideas, and your very self. Have faith in yourself and share your gifts with others through writing the best you can. If you stay true to yourself and true to your craft, you will meet the challenge and become a successful writer.

Appendix A

Treatment

"The Man Who Turned Around" or

"Turn Around"

(Secret Witness)

RACHEL FRIEDMAN BALLON, PH.D.

Night. An apartment. A man NICK BASCOLA, in middle thirties, handsome, virile and a woman, KATHY MORRIS, are in a bedroom together. He is smoking a cigarette and she is sitting next to him. He hands her a jewelry box and she opens it, taking out an expensive bracelet. She kisses him passionately, thanking him. She says he shouldn't have bought it and then she begins questioning him about where he gets so much money to buy her so many expensive gifts. This opens up further conversation about his working for his father-in-law. She asks him to quit his job and then he can leave his wife. He says it's impossible to do it now. She gets angry and demands to know when he plans to. He tries to explain that it's not that simple and not to press him for answers. He takes her in his arms telling her not to worry and he tells her how deeply he loves her. They kiss, each expressing their love.

Nicky and a woman, BETTY BASCOLA, his wife are leaving a party. It's night and they both have obviously been drinking. They are arguing as they get into a car. He starts to speed down the highway, and although you can't hear what they're saying, you can see through the window that they are still arguing. She grabs at his arm and as he tries to wrest it away the car jumps over the center divider hitting head-on a car going in the opposite direction. There is a loud crash and the cars burst into flames. Nicky is thrown free, and we see the body of Betty being trapped in the car as it is engulfed in flames.

Stock shot of the Federal Building. Interior group of offices with the name U.S. Department of Justice—Organized Crime and Racketeering Section. Inside are secretaries busy with office work. Men are at their desks, some busy with paperwork and others are talking on the phones. The attorney in charge of the local Strike Force, STEVE BRADLEY, is talking with an Inspector of the U.S. Deputy Marshalls, JOHN BURNSIDE. They are discussing the accident Nicky had when his wife was killed. They are hoping that this is the break they have been looking for and that they may now have a chance to get Nick as a witness against the Syndicate headed by his father-in-law. They have received word from an informant that his father-in-law blames Nick for the death of his daughter, and will sooner or later get revenge. Steve Bradley says that he's going to visit Nick in the hospital and try to get him to "Turn Around."

At Nick's room in the hospital, Kathy is sitting with him by his bed. His head is bandaged and he is badly battered and bruised. She tells him that she sent flowers from him to the funeral which is taking place this same day. He is visibly upset and Kathy comforts him. Steve Bradley enters and asks if he can speak to Nicky privately. He tells Nick that he is from the Justice Department. Kathy leaves looking worried. Steve tells Nick that he has it from a good source that his father-in-law is out to get him for his daughter's death. He tells Nick that he can have protection in exchange for certain information leading to the arrest and conviction of the Boss and other members of the Syndicate. Nicky tells him to get out and find another stoolie. Steve leaves telling him that he'll be in touch and to watch himself.

A man in his early sixties. Heavyset, short, and partially bald, well dressed in a black suit is standing by himself at a newly dug grave. In the background a large, black sedan is waiting for him. The man is GINO MANZANELLI, Nick's father-in-law. He is staring down at the grave of his daughter. His eyes are tear-filled. He spies flowers from Nick and a large stand. He picks up the stand and throws it from the grave. He puts other flowers on the grave. His face is angry with rage. He says, "Why couldn't it have been him instead of you?"

Bedroom in Nick's house. It's the middle of the night. Kathy reaches across the bed but it is empty. She gets up and upon hearing noises from downstairs, she goes to investigate. She overhears some loud conversation and an argument about overdue shipments and impatient customers. She hears a man telling Nicky that the boss is not too happy with his work as of late and that he better shape up. Nicky starts to defend himself. As Kathy is listening on the stairs, she trips and stumbles down some of the stairs. This noise brings Nicky and his two tough-looking companions into the hall. The two men are shocked and start too reach into their pocket when Nicky goes in front of them toward Kathy. He asks what she is doing? What happened? Kathy is nervous and scared. She starts making lame excuses for being there. Nicky suddenly realizes that the two men are looking at him angrily. He starts stumbling over his words as he attempts to introduce Kathy as an old friend of the family. The two men look at her and they knowingly catch each other's eye. Kathy and Nicky are very uncomfortable while the two men seem to be enjoying their awkwardness. As the men leave they say how sorry they were about Nicky's wife and how sad he must feel to have not been able to go to the funeral. Nicky is visibly shaken. He knows he is in real danger when they report this to his father-in-law. They exit.

Kathy rushes into his arms and starts to cry. She asks what is going on. Why is he having meetings in the middle of the night? Who were those awful looking men? What kind of business is he dealing in?

Nick tries to explain that those men were just some rough warehousemen from the docks, and when you're in the import-ing-exporting business you have to deal with all kinds of people. She begs him to quit his work now that his wife is dead. Again, he tells her he can't leave the business. She asks him if they can soon get married. She says, "I want to know what is going on, why can't you leave your business and what kind of trouble are you in?" Nicky says just to trust him and that he will marry her soon. He tells her again, how deeply he loves her and not to worry, that he'll work things out in time. Although he tries to comfort Kathy it is obvious to her that he is very frightened.

The Boss, Gino, is pounding his fist on the table of his desk. With him are the same two men who were at Nick's house. Gino is ranting and in a wild rage. He says that as of now Nicky and his girlfriend are as good as dead; that no bum and his whore will sleep in the house he bought for his daughter. He says to put out a contract on Nick, but first he wants the girl killed so that Nicky can suffer as he's suffering for his daughter. He says he plans to set Nicky up by having him come to his house for a meeting. That way Kathy will be alone in the house.

It is night. Nick is getting in the car in front of his house. He seems very nervous as he kisses Kathy good-bye. She has a dog with her that Nick recently bought for protection. He tells her he won't be long at the warehouse. She looks worried. The camera pans on a clump of trees. Behind a tree is one of the men who was with the Boss earlier. In his hand is a large knife. Kathy returns to the house with the dog by her side.

Nick drives up to a formidable-looking mansion, enclosed behind large high gates, manned by some guards. They push a button and the gates open. They motion Nicky inside. He enters the house and is sweating and chain-smoking. He is very nervous for he wonders if the men told his father-in-law about the other night. Some of the men in the room greet him casually. He goes to the bar and makes himself a drink, when his father-in-law enters. His back is turned and he misses the look of hate on

Gino's face. As Nick turns the Boss greets him with a smile and acts as if nothing has happened. Nick is visibly relieved and says it's good to see him. He starts to mention the accident, but Gino reassures him that no explanation is necessary.

Meanwhile at Nick's house the dog is pacing back and forth in front of the door. Kathy finally lets him out. She is in the kitchen and she hears a thud at the door. She opens it to let the dog in and is greeted by the body of the dog all bloodied and lying on the floor. She screams, slams the door shut, locks it and runs to the phone to call the police. The phone is dead and she frantically clicks it. The lights start to blink off and on. She searches for a candle and we hear her slamming into furniture. She finds one and runs to the den to hide behind a table. She is huddled in a corner as a man bursts in breaking down the door. She pushes the table over in front of her and he trips over it. She runs and escapes from the house. He gets up and chases her into the woods behind the house. She stumbles and he catches her. She bites him. He lets go of her and she makes her escape deeper into the woods. She stumbles and gets scratched by overhanging branches. She hides in a dense group of bushes. The man runs past Kathy. We hear a loud piercing scream as he falls into a deep ravine and is killed on the rocks below. Kathy waits for awhile and runs out of the woods to her neighbor's house where the police are called.

As Nicky drives up to his house he sees police cars all about. He rushes inside and finds Kathy crying and upset, as she relates the story of what had almost happened to her; how a man tried to kill her. She becomes hysterical and a doctor orders her to take a sedative and go to bed. A policewoman goes with her and stands outside her bedroom guarding the door. Steve Bradley drives up, and starts talking to the police about what has happened. He looks at the body they have recovered from the ravine. He shows Nicky that the man is one of the Boss's hit men. Steve asks him if he is now convinced that there is a contract out on Kathy and him. Nicky realizes that he's marked for death and he's convinced Steve is telling the truth. Steve says he can help them both in exchange for important information about how they run their operations, who they sell to and how they get drugs into the country. He also wants the names of the people involved—enough information to get convictions. Steve assures Nick that they will be fully protected by the Witness Security Program. Steve explains that Nick will get a totally new identity and a new past identity; how he'll be relocated to another city where a job will be found for him as well as a new home. He will have the protection of Personal Security Officers 24 hours a day as long as necessary. There will always be one man with him at all times. Nicky says that he doesn't want to involve Kathy in this mess. Steve says that he has no choice because she is already involved. If he leaves her they will either kill her or use her as a hostage to stop him from testifying. Nick explains that Kathy is unaware of the nature of his work. Steve says she'll have to be told right away and that she, too, will be given a new identity.

Steve and Nick talk all night and Nick starts giving some names and also a record book he has kept of all of the shipments received and those sent to other locations. Steve makes a few phone calls and starts the Witness Security Program in motion. Nick has doubts and is fearful for his and Kathy's lives, but Steve tells him that they have always been successful in protecting witnesses! Steve says they have to hurry and he calls the policewoman to awaken Kathy.

Kathy comes downstairs sleepy and completely wiped-out. Steve starts telling her about Nick's business and his working for his father-in-law in an illegal operation. Kathy is shocked but later says she suspected something like this but feels better now that she knows the truth. Steve tells her about the revenge the father-in-law wants against Nicky and that there is a contract out on him. Kathy is stunned. Steve continues to tell her there is also one on her. She can't believe it. He tells her the man tonight was hired by Nick's father-in-law and there will be another one, again. He tells Kathy that she'll have to go with Nick and that she, too, will have a new identity. Kathy asks, "What if I don't go?" Steve tells her that there really is no choice if she wants to stay alive. She stares at them in disbelief. Kathy begins to cry and says it's too much for her to digest and that she must have time to think it over. Steve says that it's impossible, they must act immediately for in a little while the Boss will have discovered the failure of his hit man and he will find another. Nicky goes to Kathy and tells her that he didn't want it to be this way for them, but that they can get a chance for a new life together and now they can be married without worrying about the business and his father-in-law, that they can go to a new town under a new identity and no one will ever interfere in their lives again. She is reassured. Steve tells them that they must hurry. He tells them to pack just a few necessary items and to get going for as of now they are under protective custody. He says by now the Boss will have found out that his plan failed. As Steve is talking the phone rings. Steve tells Nick to answer it and he listens in on the other phone. It is one of the Boss's men who tells Nick to get right over to the house for an emergency meeting. Steve nods "yes." Nick says that he'll be there in about an hour. He hangs up and looks at Steve, who says that he found out sooner than he expected and now there is no time to waste and they have to leave immediately. As they rush out of the house three moving vans pull up to it. The movers get out, enter the house and start removing all of the furniture from it and into the truck. Nick's beautiful red sportscar is also driven into the van. Within a matter of hours the vans are packed and on their way.

A long black sedan pulls up to Nick's house. The Boss is in the car. Two men get out and walk to the house. They ring the bell. They wait and get no answer. They ring again and finally kick open the door. All traces of anyone living there is gone. Gino is furious as he realizes that Nick has outsmarted him. He vows to find him.

A safe house in a lower middle class area. Nicky and Kathy are inside with John Burnside, the U.S. Marshall. He is rehearsing them on all the details of their new identity. They have new birth

certificates, drivers licenses, new medical records, new employment records, dental records, etc. All of their debts will be paid by
the Marshall through the power of attorney that Nick and Kathy
have given him. He will also close all of their charge accounts and
pay them off. All the debts will be paid from the sale of the house
and other assets they may have. Nicky and Kathy are to have no
contact *whatsoever* with any relatives or friends. Nicky says that he
has to see his parents, especially his father who isn't well. He
wants them to come to the wedding. John says it's impossible for
them to come but that he will get in touch with them and tell
them Nick is all right. Kathy says there is nobody she wants him
to contact. The quizzing continues and they are tested on their
responses. All the while they are being guarded inside and out by
men with guns dressed in street clothes.

A seedy-looking motel on a busy highway. A man steps out
of a car just as another car pulls up. It is Steve Bradley. He is meeting with Nick who continues to give him more information, more
names and dates. He tells Steve how the drugs were smuggled
into the country in the linings of leather belts and handbags
shipped from France. Steve tells him that he will be leaving town
for his new home where he will stay until he is called back to testify. They have gotten indictments against the Boss and his men
from the Grand Jury and it will be a matter of time until the trial.
Steve tells Nick his possessions are in storage and cannot be
traced because they have been moved four times under four different assumed names.

Men are again guarding the room as Steve and Nicky talk.
He tells Nick that through an informer they are planting the
story that he and Kathy will be leaving from Ontario Airport but
in reality they will leave from Burbank. Everything will be cleared
up and settled soon and they will be leaving. A job interview has
been arranged by the local Marshall through the U.S. Chamber of
Commerce in the town where Nicky will relocate. Steve tells him
he's reached Nick's parents and that his father has had another

mild stroke. Nick insists upon seeing him. Steve is firm and says it's out of the question; that Nick would not only jeopardize himself and Kathy but also his parents whose home is surely being staked out by Gino. As they are talking a big black sedan slowly enters the motel parking lot; circles around it; and finally leaves seeing only one car.

Nick and Kathy are in another safe house. They both look different in appearance. Her hair is dyed red and cut short; he has lightened his hair and has also grown a beard. They are being married by a justice of the peace, who happens to be a Marshall too. John Burnside is the best man standing up for them. During the ceremony the windows are guarded by Deputy marshalls with guns peering out of the window. The ceremony ends and they kiss. Nick says, "Hello, Mrs. Kevin Barnes." Kathy responds, "Mrs. Joyce Barnes." They kiss again.

A country road with little traffic. John, Kathy, Nick, and another deputy drive up to a deserted farm. The barn door opens and they drive in. Inside there is another car. They change cars with the two other deputies, one of whom is dressed exactly like Nicky. Steve Bradley shakes hands with Nick saying good-bye. He tells him that he must follow all of John's orders and they'll be safe for they haven't lost a secret witness yet. He gets into the other car and drives away heading toward the Ontario Airport.

Soon a black sedan are following them. Steve and his deputies smile as they realize their plan has worked. Kathy, Nick, and John are heading in the opposite direction, to another airport.

When the deputies arrive at the airport there are other Deputy Marshalls already there, dressed as skycaps, mechanics, and cabdrivers. There is a shootout and the deputy dressed as Nick is hit, but not seriously. Soon police cars converge and the men following realize they have been set-up. They are arrested and the black sedan tries to make a getaway. Steve chases them and shoots out a tire. They crash. The driver and Gino are arrested.

The car with John and Nick and Kathy get to the other airport. The baggage is taken through by personal security officers. Nick, John, and Kathy board the plane at the last minute through a back entrance.

City in West Virginia. They drive up to a small street of tract houses. Inside the furniture is very sparse and cheap-looking. Nick looks around disgruntled. He is not used to this kind of life and hadn't anticipated anything this simple. He starts to complain to John, with whom he has established a good relationship, and John kids him telling him it's better than a home six feet under. They start to review more information about their new identity. John and Nick play some gin while Kathy makes dinner. The phone rings and it's the local Marshall telling them a job interview has been set up for Nick to have tomorrow.

Nick is interviewed by the head of a chain of wholesale stores on the order of Zody's or Sears. Nick will work as a salesman in the import department. The man tells him that no one knows anything about his background or past.

Nick is working in the department. Every once in awhile he sees the same customer day after day in his department. He becomes very nervous. Tells John who checks the man out. It's learned that he is slightly retarded and visits the store for lack of anything else to do.

Kathy's and Nick's neighbors try to befriend them but, though they are polite they do not respond to a relationship. It is hard for Nick to adjust to this lack of money when he has been used to wealth and a different life socially. Kathy is satisfied in being married and with Nick. They still have the protection of John Burnside. He tells Nick that they will soon be leaving for Los Angeles, where he is to testify for the prosecution.

They return to Los Angeles. Nick tells the Marshall that he wants to call his parents to see how his father is doing. They find a pay phone and he makes the call. As Nick talks his face becomes tense. He says that he'll be there right away. He hangs up and tells

John that he has to go to the bathroom. At the garage where they stopped to use the phone, he goes inside and waits for the right moment, when John's back is turned he rushes out and takes a car and heads toward his parents' home.

We see the call being monitored by Gino and some of his men. They quickly call the hit man and tell him Nick is on his way.

Nick drives to his house. He parks the car a block away and furtively tries to get to his home unnoticed. As he nears the house he sees he is being followed. There is a chase scene. The hit man is gaining on Nick who is unarmed. He runs down an alleyway which is a dead end. The man gains on him. He sneers at Nick saying, "This is what we do to stoolies." He raises his gun at Nick's face and there is a gunshot, but it is the hit man who falls. He is killed by the Marshall who followed Nick home.

Nick is swiftly driven to another safe house where John tells him he was stupid and could have gotten killed.

Stock shot of Federal Building. Courtroom spectators rush to find a seat after first being searched. Deputies are guarding all entrances. At the defense table is Gino and his associates and their respective attorneys. At the prosecution table is Steve Bradley and his assistant attorneys. A feeling of tension pervades.

A garbage truck arrives at the back entrance of the building. As it passes the man accompanying the driver has a concealed gun in his lap and is looking at the rooftops of nearby buildings. As expected, there are figures standing all around. They are Deputy Marshalls looking for hit men.

In one of the garbage cans they remove from the truck is Nicky concealed inside it. He gets out and is accompanied by the two men dressed as garbage collectors. Inside they take off their suits that collectors wear, and they accompany Nick, one on either side of him to the side entrance of the courtroom. All eyes focus upon Nicky. He and Gino's eyes meet. Gino glares at him. There is a stirring in the courtroom.

Television set is showing a commentator delivering the evening news. We hear him excitedly announcing that the head of the local drug ring, Gino Manzanelli and some of his associates have been found guilty and that the prosecution has won their case, by presenting a witness who testified against them. He continues saying that they tried to get the witness to interview him, but there is now no trace of him and that it seems he has disappeared into thin air. Picture on TV of Nick covering his face with his hands and with the help of the Marshalls on either side of him.

As we hear the commentator still talking about the case we see a catering truck pull up to a commercial plane. Three attendants take the food aboard—they are Nick, Kathy, and John Burnside, U.S. Marshall. Another Secret Witness Saved!

Appendix B

Query Letter to an Agent

March 1, 1995

John Doe
Doe, Weeks and Day
100 Fifth Avenue, 10th Floor
New York, New York 00102

Dear Mr. Doe:

I have just completed *Mercy on Trial*, a novel that appeals to the public's never-ending fascination with mercy killing and the courtroom drama of murder trials.

The retirement dream of David Neal, a once-prominent Professor Emeritus of Psychology at a small Michigan college, is smashed when the publisher of his earlier academic works rejects his latest book for which he held high hopes. Unhappy and depressed at seventy-five, David's life is empty and meaningless. Increasingly emotionally dependent on Lu, is wife of fifty years, David is preoccupied with the fear that she will die before him, leaving him to face his bleak life alone.

David's despair is aggravated by estrangement from his only child, Betty, a hard-driving trial partner in a prominent Detroit law firm, who refuses to forgive her father for his old extramarital affair that inflicted great heartache on her mother, Lu. Betty's rebellious

seventeen-year-old son, Eddie, has run away from his domineering
mother and lives with his grandparents, Lu and David. Depressed
and self-absorbed, David's relationship with Eddie is distant. David
is sure that the teenager loves Lu and not him.

Suddenly Lu is felled by a stroke and lies in a coma, sus-
tained by a respirator. David maintains a constant vigil at Lu's
bedside believing that she will recover and that they will resume
their life together, even if it means dressing her himself and push-
ing her around campus in a wheelchair. But slowly he comes to
the agonizing realization that Lu is in a permanent vegetative
state. As her coma nears 60 days, Eddie blurts out the brutal
truth: "Grandmother will never get well. She would rather be
dead than the way she is now."

Night after night, David meditates by the frozen river, trying
to decide what to do. He puts his pistol to his head, but, repelled
by the thought of leaving Lu helpless and alone, he fires the gun
harmlessly into the sky. Finally David asks the family doctor to
end Lu's life by turning off her respirator. He plans to kill himself
when the deed is done. But because David and Lu have failed to
sign living wills, the law requires that Betty, as their daughter,
give her consent. David pleads for her approval, but she refuses to
consent to what she calls the "murder" of her mother.

After agonizing for days, David takes matters into his own
hands by turning off Lu's respirator, killing her. His attempt to
shoot himself is foiled by the nurse who rushes into the hospital
room.

Fred Cain, a politically ambitious prosecutor, brings murder
charges against David, who is defended without fee by the
famous African-American lawyer, Joseph Thomas Jefferson. The
trial attracts national TV and print coverage. Despite Jefferson's
skillful defense, David fears he will be convicted. The trial's dark-
est hour comes when his own daughter testifies against him. He
dreads facing the rest of his life in the penitentiary.

David feels wholly inadequate in attempting to justify his
actions to the jury, but the momentum of the trial toward cer-

tain conviction is reversed by the surprise appearance of his grandson, Eddie, who has run away to join the Marines. Taking the witness stand in his full dress Marine uniform, Eddie explains to the jury that his grandfather had little choice but to end his grandmother's life: "If Grandfather had not done it, I would have," he testifies.

Mercy on Trial explores the legal, psychological, and moral issues of mercy killing through the testimony of the witnesses, the attorneys' arguments, and the acrimonious debate among the divided and troubled jurors. After days of deliberation, the jury moves from eight to four for conviction to eleven to one for acquittal. Risking all, David turns down a plea bargain, but his hope for vindication is dashed when the jury announces that it is deadlocked. Despite pressure from the other eleven who now wish to acquit David, one juror insists on a guilty verdict and David faces the perils of a retrial. But when the jury is polled in open court, a startling and unprecedented event changes the anticipated outcome of the trial.

Mercy on Trial draws on my extensive experience as a trial lawyer. Many of my writings on legal, economic, and political matters have been published in periodicals such as *The Wall Street Journal, Michigan Law Review, Prentice Hall Professional Corporations Service, Los Angeles Bar Journal,* and newspapers and magazines in both the U.K. and the U.S. My comments on business success and commitment were included in an article in *Reader's Digest* and in my interview on ABC's *Wall Street Week.*

Geoffrey Fieger, Esq., the lawyer for Dr. Jack Kevorkian, has provided me with legal research.

If this project is of interest, I shall be happy to provide you with sample chapters or with the entire completed manuscript.

Very truly yours,

Wendell B. Will

Appendix C

Book Proposal

"Never Be Taken for Granted . . . Again!
Getting the Respect and Recognition You Deserve
at Work, Love, and Home"

SUSAN BERK

TABLE OF CONTENTS

INTRODUCTION

During the 1980s personal sales and marketing books were hot sellers. They had titles like "How to Market Yourself," "How to Sell Your Ideas," "How to Influence and Persuade," "How to Present Yourself With Impact." When I see these books in people's personal libraries or in their offices, I always ask what they've learned and what they've done differently as a result of reading these books. And the inevitable answer is: "Well, I haven't done anything yet, but I really saw myself in the book." Or . . . "the author was great, she exactly identified the dilemma I'm in at home or work."

Why haven't these readers been able to make the leap from recognizing the problem to actually doing something about it? It isn't that the books aren't filled with good solid marketing approaches and sales techniques and it isn't that the readers aren't capable of carrying through on the good ideas. I've found that even when you give a person all of these skills, they still can't be enthusiastic and market or sell themselves because *they don't believe in the product*! They don't believe in themselves! They read the books and hear the success stories, but deep down they always feel as though the people in the examples are just a little bit smarter or a little more intelligent than they are. It's as though others had something in them—a spark which allowed them to identify the problem, read the techniques, and then go out and change. Something most readers feel they don't have!

Never Be Taken for Granted . . . Again! Getting the Respect and Recognition You Deserve at Work, Love and Home deals with first things first. It starts with showing you how to recognize and articulate your own value and then gives you techniques on how to stop getting taken for granted by others! This is a book about getting beyond one's personal fear of being "found out" and learning techniques which will overcome insecurity and self-doubt. It works because it teaches you to market yourself from the INSIDE out, rather than just applying clever techniques to your external life. It's a unique blend of psychology and marketing skills and allows the reader to understand their behavioral choices and how each choice can trigger predetermined reactions from others. One by one it eliminates the negative actions people cling to in an attempt to gain recognition. The reader will learn why these actions are doomed to fail and how even these inevitable failures—no matter how often they're repeated, serve to validate self-doubt—creating a destructive cycle which is continuously reinforced.

Never Be Taken for Granted . . . Again! Getting The Respect And Recognition You Deserve at Work, Love and Home presents easy-to-use steps for becoming a player rather than a bystander in your own life. It helps you, the reader, celebrate the job of participating and not just sitting on the sidelines. It is not another clever self-help book, but rather a reality-based system for getting what everyone wants and needs—respect and recognition. Susan Berk, a management consultant has given her Visibility Workshops to thousands of professionals, CEOs, secretaries, engineers, managers, civic leaders, lawyers, business executives, and consultants. Rachel Ballon, a licensed psychotherapist saw the overwhelming need that people from all walks of life have for wanting recognition and appreciation and took these techniques—expanded and refined them—to use in conjunction with psychotherapy in her private practice. They brought immediate positive results and had an especially powerful impact on patients who felt victimized and taken for granted by people in their lives.

In addition to using them in their private practice, these techniques proved so powerful that Rachel has combined them with her background as a screenwriter and writing teacher to help writers, directors, producers and actors, and other creative professionals working in the entertainment industry get professional respect and recognition in a difficult business.

In bringing together this unique collaboration of psychology, image marketing, and motivational training, Susan and

Rachel have developed a new concept to teach people to stop being taken for granted and get recognition.

They teach people how to market themselves from the INSIDE OUT. They deal with strategies for overcoming the most frustrating aspects people daily encounter—not getting listened to, not getting recognition or respect. Each chapter in the book takes the reader beyond the passive preaching and platitudes, to the active techniques for getting recognition. They'll learn how to create and market a more positive self-image and how to present good ideas so that others will stand up and pay attention!

Appendix D

Synopsis for a TV Movie-of-the-Week

"The Love Game"

RACHEL FRIEDMAN BALLON, PH.D. and NAOMI FELDMAN

The Love Game is a story of relationships: their rewards, their difficulties, their pleasures, their pain. It is the story of four women who have grown up in the 1950s and who are confronted with the values of the 1980s. These women and their husbands become victims of their own or their mates' mid-life crises. The four women are good friends and tennis partners.

The Love Game is the story of: Cassie and Jack Grayson, who divorce when Jack leaves her for a much younger woman. Diana and Arnold Philips, who live "somewhere between marriage and divorce." Diana takes a younger lover and leaves Arnold, but returns to a marriage which is emotionally unfulfilling, when her lover is unable to make a commitment to her. Mia and Ben Reynolds, whose marriage is disrupted when Mia, about to turn forty, leaves Ben for the promise of a dazzling career and an exciting future which never materializes. Helen and Harry Burns, who are married in name only, although Helen adores her husband. She is the least likely of the four women to survive and emerge as a winner, who achieves success on her own, as she eventually does.

The Love Game is a story about women and their families. It involves their loves, their children, their lack of communication, their intimacies, and their feelings of alienation. Each family undergoes it's own upheaval as the women are either defeated by or survive the changes the years have brought.

Appendix E

Script Format for a Movie

"Hit or Miss"

**RACHEL FRIEDMAN BALLON, PH.D. and
ADRIENNE FAYNE**

<u>FADE IN:</u>

<u>UNDER CREDITS:</u>

INT. CORRIDOR - DAY

CHARLENE PATTERSON, early thirties, wearing a large scarf, rushes down the hall CRYING. PETE PATTERSON, her husband, middle forties, a burly construction worker storms down the hall beside her. They stop as they reach a door. She CRIES LOUDER.

CLOSE on door

NORMAN SHORTMAN, M.D.
A MEDICAL CORPORATION
PLASTIC AND RECONSTRUCTIVE SURGERY

INT. OFFICE - DAY

A modern waiting room filled with patients. One woman has two black eyes and a partially bandaged nose. A man wears a huge bandage around his face. The Pattersons enter and hurry to reception window. Charlene is SOBBING.

INT. EXAM ROOM - DAY

It is a typical examination room of a plastic surgeon. There is a chair in the center and an exam table off to the side. Several blown up photos line the wall. They are all different shots of before and after noses, eyes, breasts, and hips of a young woman. We CLOSE in on a gorgeous young woman, LISA WHITNEY, 29, facing the camera. She is the woman in the shots. She starts to slowly unfasten her bra and takes it off, revealing the two most perfect breasts—rounded, firm, uplifted and full. A doctor wearing a white jacket, NORMAN SHORTMAN, M.D. mid forties, attractive, stands gazing upon them.

> NORMAN
> Fantastic. They're absolutely beautiful.
> I've done it again.

He steps toward her and with both hands cupped he embraces each breast tenderly. Lisa smiles and puts her arms about him as the two passionately kiss.

> LISA
> How can I thank you, darling?

> NORMAN
> You know how to thank me.

They are locked together hot and heavy as they move toward examining table.

                                                    CUT TO:

INT. OFFICE - LATER

Norman is lying on top of Lisa and they have just finished making love on the examination table. Phone BUZZES. Lisa pushes him off and he lands on the floor. As Lisa starts fixing her clothes, Norman gets off floor and tries to grab her. Phone BUZZES again. Norman ignores it.

                        NORMAN
            Baby, I love you.

                        LISA
            I love you too, but I can't wait forever.

                        NORMAN
            (pulling her toward him)
            You won't have to.

                        LISA
            Oh, have you told Brenda that you want a divorce?

PHONE RINGS again. Norman rushes to answer and gets twisted among the cord and his pants fall down. WOMAN'S VOICE OVER INTERCOM.

                        RECEPTIONIST (V.O.)
            Dr. Shortman, you better see Mr. & Mrs. Patterson
            right away. They're creating a disturbance in the
            office.

                    NORMAN
          Be right there.

                     LISA
          Norman, I'm giving you until New Years
          to leave your wife.

Receptionist BUZZES again. Norman REACTS.

              RECEPTIONIST (V.O.)
          You better hurry before they tear up the place.

                     LISA
          Calm them down, before you have another
          malpractice suit.
                    (beat)
          Don't forget . . . New Year's.

Norman puts his white doctor's coat on and EXITS.

                                        CUT TO:

INT. EXAMINATION ROOM - LATER

Pete paces back and forth. He punches his fist into his open hand
as he walks. Charlene sits with her back to the CAMERA WHIM-
PERING into a handkerchief. Norman opens the door and enters.
He smiles and slaps Pete on the back.

                  CHARLENE
                  (screaming)
          Look at my breasts.

CLOSE ON BREASTS

She opens her coat and is wearing a tight sweater. One breast hangs down and the other sticks straight out.

> NORMAN
> (soothing her)
> Charlene, don't worry—I'll fix everything.
> How do you like your sexy, new lips.
> (beat)
> Pretty sensuous, aren't they?

He starts to walk over to her, when Pete grabs Norman by the collar and pulls him over to his wife, who by now is WAILING. Pete takes Charlene's face and turns it for Norman to see.

CLOSE ON CHARLENE'S FACE

Her lips are double their size, her eyes have a surprised look and are opened wide-eyed.

> PETE
> Lips, you call these lips. They look
> like a pig's ass . . . .

Charlene WAILS LOUDER.

> PETE CONT'D)
> . . . her eyes are bugging out of her head
> and her breasts look like a cow's udder.

Pete punches him in the jaw and Norman falls backward to the floor.

NORMAN
Don't get excited. I can fix her up like new.
At no charge to you.

Patterson reaches down and makes a fist into Norman's face.

PETE
You'll never get to butcher my wife again.

Sources

Protect your manuscript by registering it with the copyright office in Washington, D.C.:

Copyright Office
Library of Congress
Washington, D.C. 20559
(703) 557-Info

The Writers Guild of America

The Writers Guild of America with branches in the East and West, represent screenwriters, television writers, and radio writers. The one-time-only initiation fee is $1,500 for the West division and $1,000 for the East. Quarterly dues are $25 and $12.50, respectively. The guild arbitrates when there are disputes regarding a writer's credits and helps with contract negotiations. It has strict rules about what its members may accept as a minimum wage and what companies they can write for. It sets these minimum rates for sitcoms, one-hour episodic dramas, feature films, and television movies, and specifies the residual for reruns.

The WGA, West puts out a monthly magazine called *The Journal*, filled with resources for writers, interesting articles, and news about the latest deals, disputes, and innovations in the entertainment industry. The cost of a yearly subscription for nonmembers is $40. For more information, write to *The Journal* at the following address:

> Writers Guild of America West
> 7000 West Third Street
> Los Angeles, California 90048
> (213) 951-4000

> Writers Guild of America East
> 555 West Fifty-seventh Street, Suite 1230
> New York, NY 10019
> (212) 767-7800

To protect your screenplay, television script, sitcom, hour episode, or feature film, register it with the guild (either branch). Call for the cost. After your property is registered, it will be protected for five years, and then you must renew.

Periodicals for Writers

> *Kirkus Review* (Subscription Service)
> 200 Park Avenue South, 11th Floor
> New York, New York 10003
> (212) 777-4554
> Fax: (212) 979-1352

> *Publishers Weekly*
> 249 West Seventeenth Street
> New York, New York 10011

> *Writer's Digest*
> 1507 Dana Avenue
> Cincinnati, Ohio 45207

The Writer
120 Boylston Street
Boston, Massachusettes 02116

Writers and Poets
72 Spring Street
New York, New York 10012

Trade Publications

Daily Variety
5700 Wilshire Boulevard
Hollywood, California 90036

Drama-Logue
1456 North Gordon Street
Hollywood, California 90038
(213) 464-5079

The Hollywood Reporter
5055 Wilshire Boulevard
Los Angeles, California 90036

Weekly Variety
5700 Wilshire Boulevard
Los Angeles, California 90036

The Hollywood Scriptwriter
1626 North Wilcox Avenue
Los Angeles, California 90028

Script
5683 Sweet Air Road
Baldwin, Maryland 21013-0007

Entertainment Industry Organizations

Directors Guild of America
7920 Sunset Boulevard
Los Angeles, California 90046
(310) 289-2000

Producers Guild of America
400 South Beverly Drive, Suite 211
Beverly Hills, California 90212
(310) 557-0807

Screen Actors Guild
5757 Wilshire Boulevard
Los Angeles, California 90036
(213) 954-1600

Writers Guild of America West
7000 West Third Street
Los Angeles, California 90048
(213) 951-4000

Sundance Institute
225 Santa Monica Blvd., 8th Floor
Santa Monica, CA 90401

Academy of Television Arts and Sciences
5220 Lankershim Boulevard
North Hollywood, California 91601
(818) 754-2800

Academy of Motion Picture Arts and Sciences
8949 Wilshire Boulevard
Beverly Hills, California 90211
(310) 247-3000

American Federation of Television and Radio Artists
6922 Hollywood Boulevard
Los Angeles, California 90028
(213) 634-8100

Independent Feature Project/West
1625 Olympic Boulevard
Santa Monica, California 90404
(310) 475-4379

Journalism

Professional Organizations

American Society of Journalists and Authors
1501 Broadway, Suite 302
New York, New York 10036
(212) 997-0947

The society, a professional organization for nonfiction free-lance magazine and newspaper writers, has meetings throughout the year for members, as well as some that are open to the public. It also has an annual conference.

Periodicals for Journalists

Folio. The Magazine Business.

Journalism Career and Scholarship Guide. Published by Dow Jones Newspaper Fund. Has directory of journalism schools. You can obtain a free copy by writing to P.O. Box 300, Princeton, New Jersey 08543.

Periodicals for Writers

Publishers Weekly. Book publishing.

Subject Guide To Books In Print. In most libraries.

Editor And Publisher Yearbook. In libraries.

Technical Writing

The following are resources for technical writers:

Southern Illinois University
Division of Continuing Education
Carbondale, Illinois 62901

Society of Technical Communications
815 Fifteenth Street, NW, Suite 506
Washington, D.C. 20005

Film Schools

The following are well-known film schools where the competition is very tough and the prestige is very high:

New York University
Tisch School of The Arts
721 Broadway
New York, New York 10003

University of California, Los Angeles
Department of Film and Television
405 Hilgard Avenue
Los Angeles, California 90024

AFI Center For Advanced
Film and Television Studies
2021 North Western Avenue
Los Angeles, California 90027

University of Southern California
School of Cinema and Television
University Park
Los Angeles, California 90089

The following source offers information about screenplay contests:

Writer's Aide
1685 South Colorado Boulevard, Suite 237
Denver, Colorado 80222

The following is a partial list of contests for screenwriters:

Tisch School of The Arts
721 Broadway, Sixth Floor
New York, New York 10003-6807

Diane Thomas Contest
UCLA Extension, Writer's Program
10995 Le Conte Avenue
Los Angeles, California 90024-2883

Christopher Columbus Awards
433 North Camden Drive
Beverly Hills, Cailfornia 90210

Nicholl Fellowship Competition
Academy of Motion Picture Arts and Sciences
8949 Wilshire Boulevard
Beverly Hills, California 90211-1972

Disney Fellow
Nevada Motion Picture Division
Screenwriters Competition
555 East Washington Avenue, Suite 5400
Las Vegas, Nevada 89101

The Writer's Network Screenplay Competition
289 South Robertson Boulevard, Suite 465
Beverly Hills, California 90211

Writing Grants and Fellowships

Anthology Film Art Fund
32–34 Second Avenue
New York, New York 10003

Black American Filmmakers Grants Program
Western States Black Research Center
3617 Montclair Street
Los Angeles, California 90018

Disney Fellowship Program
Disney Studios
500 South Buena Vista Street
Burbank, California 91521-0880

Film Arts Foundation (Must be resident of San Francisco)
346 Ninth Street, Second Floor
San Francisco, California 94013

James A. Michener Fellowship
Texas Center for Writers
Mail Code S5401
University of Texas
Austin, Texas 78713-7330

National Endowment for The Arts
Film-Video Grants (Deadline: October 29)
1100 Pennsylvania Avenue, NW
Washington, D.C. 20506

Writing Seminars

Writer's Connection
P.O. Box 24770
San Jose, California 95154-4770

Mr. Robert McKee
Two Arts, Inc.
12021 Wilshire Boulevard
Los Angeles, California 90025

Hollywood Film Institute
Mr. Dov S-S Simens
5225 Wilshire Boulevard
Los Angeles, California 90036

Correspondence Courses In Writing

"Write at Home"
Feature Screenwriting Correspondence Course
4470 Sunset Boulevard, Suite 179
Hollywood, California 90027
(213) 664-4851

You can also find schools that offer correspondence courses in *The Writer's Digest* or *The Writer.*

Writing Organizations

Pen American Center
568 Broadway
New York, New York 10012
(212) 334-1660

Pen Center USA West
672 South Lafayette Park Place, Suite 41
Los Angeles, California 90057
(213) 365-8500

To become a member of Pen, you must have published one or two books. There are different criteria for playwrights, screenwriters, and others in associated writing fields. Members receive a quarterly Pen newsletter, and many chapters offer monthly talks or seminars for members.

National Writers Association
1450 South Havana, Suite 424
Aurora, Colorado 80012
(303) 751-7844

The National Writers Association is open to professional and nonprofessional writers.

Author's Guild
330 West Forty-second Street
New York, New York 10036
(212) 563-5904

The Author's Guild is an organization of professional magazine and book writers. It will provide writers with information on copyright, contracts, and other issues. Members are required to have published a book with a recognized publishing house within seven years of applying for membership. For magazine writers, the requirement is publication of several magazine articles or fiction pieces in a general-interest magazine within eighteen months of applying for membership.

Poetry Society of America
15 Gramercy Park
New York, New York 10003
(212) 254-9628

This Poetry Society of America publishes a newsletter and offers discounts at readings and seminars to its members. Poetry lovers—whether writers or readers—can join.

Society of Authors' Representatives
10 Astor Place, Third Floor
New York, New York, 10003

The Society of Authors' Representatives will send you a free booklet explaining what role an agent will play in your life as a playwright. Include a self-addressed, stamped envelope.

Sources for Playwrights

Dramatists Sourcebook
Theatre Communications Group
355 Lexington Avenue
New York, New York 10017

This sourcebook lists marketing venues for playwrights and agents.

NEA Theater Program Fellowship for Playwrights
1100 Pennsylvania Avenue, NW
Washington, D.C. 20506

The National Endowment for the Arts gives grants to professional playwrights whose plays have been produced.

The Dramatists Guild
1501 Broadway, Suite 701
New York, New York 10036
(212) 398-9366

The Dramatists Guild offers memberships for eligible play-wrights. Associate members need not have a produced play. Active members include writers who have been produced in regional theater, on Broadway, or in an off-Broadway house. It offers many benefits and helps playwrights with under-standing their rights.

Theatres

The following is a partial list of theatres throughout the United States:

American Conservatory Theater
450 Geary Street
San Francisco, California 94102

American Place Theatre
111 West Forty-sixth Street
New York, New York 10036

American Repertory Theatre
64 Brattle Street
Cambridge, Massachusettes 02138

National Ten-Minute Play Contest
Actors Theatre of Louisville
36 West Main Street
Louisville, Kentucky 40202

Arena Stage
Sixth and Maine Avenue, SW
Washington, D.C. 20024

Berkeley Repertory Theatre
2025 Addison Street
Berkeley, California 94704

The Cast Theatre
804 North El Centro Avenue
Hollywood, California 90038

Children's Theatre Company
2400 Third Avenue South
Minneapolis, Minnesota 55404

Denver Center Theatre Company
1050 Thirteenth Street
Denver, Colorado 80204

Guthrie Theatre
725 Vineland Place
Minneapolis, Minnesota 55503

Illinois Theatre
400A Lakewood Boulevard
Park Forest, Illinois 60466

Madison Repertory Theatre
211 State Street
Madison, Wisconsin 53703

Mark Taper Forum
135 North Grand Avenue
Los Angeles, California 90012

National Jewish Theater
5050 West Church Street
Skokie, Illinois 60077

New York Shakespeare Festival
Public Theatre
425 Lafayette Street
New York, New York 10003

Odyssey Theatre Ensemble
2055 South Sepulveda Boulevard
Los Angeles, California 90025

La Jolla Playhouse
Box 12039
La Jolla, California 92039

Old Globe Theatre
Box 2171
San Diego, California 92112

Oregon Shakespeare Festival
Box 158
Ashland, Oregon 97520

Long Whorf Theatre
222 Sargent Drive
New Haven, Connecticut 06511

Philadelphia Theatre Company
The Bourse Building, Suite 735
21 South Fifth Street
Philadelphia, Pennsylvania 19106

Portland Repertory Theatre
2 World Trade Center
25 South West Salmon Street
Portland, Oregon 97204

Seattle Repertory Theatre
155 Mercer Street
Seattle, Washington 98109

South Coast Repertory
Box 2197
Costa Mesa, California 92628

Steppenwolf Theatre Co.
2851 North Halsted Street
Chicago, Illinois 60657

Tennessee Repertory Theatre
427 Chestnut Street
Nashville, Tennessee 37203

Vineyard Theatre
108 East Fifteenth Street
New York, New York 10003

Woolly Mammoth Theatre Company
1401 Church Street, NW
Washington, D.C. 20005

Yale Repertory Theatre
Box 1903A
Yale Station
New Haven, Connecticut 06520

Contests for Playwrights

The following is a partial list:

American Musical Theatre Festival Competition
Box S-3565
Carmel, California 93921
Fee. Full-length musicals. Deadline: December 31.

Lucille Ball Festival of New Comedy
American Vaudeville
Box 2619, Times Square Station
New York, New York 10108
Short comedies. Deadline: October 15.

Beverly Hills Theatre Guild
Julie Harris Playwright Award
2815 North Beachwood Drive
Los Angeles, California 90068
Full-length plays. Deadline: November 1.

California Playwrights Competition
South Coast Repertory
Box 2197
Costa Mesa, California 92628
Full-length plays open to California residents.
Deadline: November 1 or later.

The Richard Rodgers Production Award
American Academy and Institute of Arts and Letters
633 West Fifteenth Street
New York, New York 10032
Musicals. Deadline: November 2

Writers' Organizations of General Interest

The Writers Alliance
12 Skylark Lane
Stony Brook, New York 11790

National Writers Association
1450 Havana, Suite 424
Aurora, Colorado 80012

Authors League of America
234 West Forty-fourth Street
New York, New York 10024

Association of American Publishers
220 East Twenty-third Street
New York, New York 10010

Children's Book Council
508 Broadway
New York, New York 10012

Pen American Center
568 Broadway
New York, New York 10012

Book Stores for Scripts

Script City
8033 Sunset Boulevard
Suite 1500-RB
Los Angeles, California 90049
(213) 871-0707

This is a mail-order house that offers thousands of film and
TV scripts, books on screenwriting, and software.

Samuel French Theatre and Film Books
7623 Sunset Boulevard
Los Angeles, California 90046

This bookstore specializes in published plays, films, and TV
scripts, scriptwriting books, and software dealing with writing, directing, producing, and acting.

Larry Edmunds
6644 Hollywood Boulevard
Los Angeles, California 90028

Specializes in all types of books on film and TV writing,
including production, trade magazines, and scripts.

Enterprise Printers and Stationers
7401 Sunset Boulevard
Los Angeles, California 90046
(213) 876-3530

Stocks all types of release forms, contracts, and scriptwriting
books.

Literary Agents

The following is a partial list of literary agents, mostly for books:

Anita Diamant Literary Agency
310 Madison Avenue
New York, New York 10017

The Jeff Herman Agency
500 Greenwich Street
Suite 501 C
New York, New York 10013

Lowenstein Associates
121 West Twenty-seventh Street, Suite 601
New York, New York 10001

Carol Mann Literary Agency
55 Fifth Avenue
New York, New York 10003

Margaret McBride Literary Agency
7744 Fay Avenue, Suite 201
La Jolla, California 92037

William Morris Agency
1350 Avenue of the Americas
New York, New York 10019

William Morris Agency
151 El Camino Drive
Beverly Hills, California 90212

Michael Larsen/Elizabeth Pomoda Literary Agents
1029 Jones Street
San Francisco, California 94109

The Charlotte Gusse Literary Agency
10532 Blythe Avenue
Los Angeles, California 90064

Sandra Dijkstra Literary Agency
1155 Camino del Mar
Del Mar, California 92014

James Levine Communications
330 Seventh Avenue, Fourteenth Floor
New York, New York 10001

Linda Chester Agency
630 Fifth Avenue, Suite 2258
New York, NY 10111

Documentaries

International Documentary Association
1551 South Robertson Boulevard, Suite 201
Los Angeles, California 90035-4257

This organization promotes nonfiction film and videos and supports the efforts of documentary filmmakers worldwide.

Writers Career

Donie Nelson
Carrer Strategies for Writers
10736 Jefferson Boulevard, Suite 508
Culver City, California 90230-4969

Smart Girls Productions
P.O. Box 1896
Los Angeles, California 90078

This organization sends out query-letter mailings for writers to agents and producers.

Bibliography

Allen, Linda Buchanan. *Write and Sell Your Free-Lance Article.* Boston: The Writer, Inc., 1991.

Appelbaum, Judith. *How to Get Happily Published.* New York: Harper Perennial, 1992.

Baker, Samm Sinclair. *Writing Nonfiction that Sells.* Cincinnati: Writer's Digest Books, 1986.

Begley, Adam. *Between Agents: A Writer's Guide.* New York: Penguin Books, 1992.

Bivins, Thomas. *Handbook for Public Relations Writing.* Lincolnwood: NTC Business Books, 1988.

Blake, Gary and Robert W. Bly. *The Elements of Business Writing.* New York: MacMillan Publishing Co., 1991.

Brande, Dorothea. *Becoming a Writer.* Los Angeles: Jeremy P. Tarcher, 1981.

Brooks, Terri. *A Handbook on Writing and Selling Nonfiction.* New York: St. Martin's Press, 1989.

Burack, Sylvia K. (Ed.) *The Writer's Handbook.* Boston: The Writer, Inc., 1990.

Dramatists Sourcebook. New York: Theatre Communications Group (Annual).

Egri, Lajos. *The Art of Dramatic Writing.* New York: Simon and Schuster, 1979.

Elbow, Peter. *Writing With Power: Techniques for Mastering the Writing Process.* Oxford: Oxford University Press, 1981.

Epstein, Connie C. *The Art of Writing for Children.* Hamden: Archon Books, 1991.

Field, Syd. *Screenplay.* New York: Dell, 1984.

Freedman, Helen Rosengren and Karen Frieger. *The Writer's Guide to Magazine Markets: Non-Fiction.* New York: Plume, 1983.

Gearing, Philip J. and Evelyn V. Brunson. *Breaking Into Print: How to Get Your Work Published.* Englewood Cliffs: Prentice-Hall, Inc., 1977.

Gee, Robin. (Ed.) *Novel & Short Story Writer's Market.* Cincinnati: Writer's Digest Books, 1991.

Hall, Roger A. *Writing Your First Play.* Boston: Focal Press, 1991.

Heffron, Jack. (Ed.) *The Best Writing on Writing.* Cincinnati: Story Press, 1994.

Herbert, Katherine Atwell. *Writing Scripts Hollywood Will Love: An Insider's Guide to Film and Television Scripts That Sell.* New York: Allworth Press, 1994.

Highsmith, Patricia. *Plotting and Writing Suspense Fiction.* London: Poplar Press Ltd, 1987.

Jerome, Judson. *On Being A Poet*. Cincinnati: Writer's Digest Books, 1984.

Kenles, Barbara L. *Basic Magazine Writing*. Cincinnati: Writer's Digest Books, 1986.

Konner, Linda. *How to Be Successfully Published in Magazines*. New York: St. Martin's Press, 1990.

Lewis, Claudia. *Writing for Young Children*. New York: Penguin Books, 1981.

MacManus, Yvonne. *You Can Write a Romance and Get It Published*. New York: Pocket Books, 1983.

McLarn, Jack Clinton. *Writing Part-Time for Fun and Money*. Wilmington: Enterprise Publishing, Inc., 1978.

Perret, Gene. *Comedy Writing Step By Step*. Hollywood: Samuel French, 1990.

Polking, Kirk. (Ed.) *Beginning Writer's Answer Book*. Cincinnati: Writer's Digest, 1993.

Roberts, E.M. *The Children's Picture Book*. Cincinnati: Writer's Digest Books, 1981.

Sandman, Larry. (Ed.) *A Guide to Greeting Card Writing*. Cincinnati: Writer's Digest Books,   1980.

Shamos, Laura. *Playwriting for Theater, Film and TV*. Crozet: Betterway Publications, Inc., 1991.

Seger, Linda. *The Art of Adaptation: Turning Fact & Fiction into Film*. New York: Henry Holt & Co., 1992.

Sides, Charles H. *How to Write & Present Technical Information.* Phoenix: The Oryx Press, 1991.

Smiley, Sam. *Playwriting: The Structure of Action.* New York: Prentice-Hall, Inc., 1971.

Spender, Stephen. *The Making of a Poem.* New York: W.W. Norton & Company, Inc., 1961.

Staurt, Linda. *Getting Your Script Through the Hollywood Maze.* Los Angeles: Acrobat Books, 1993.

Treat, Lawrence. (Ed.) *Mystery Writer's Handbook.* Cincinnati: Writer's Digest Books, 1976.

Wilson, John M. *The Complete Guide to Magazine Article Writing.* Cincinnati: Writer's Digest Books, 1993.

Wimberly, Darryl and Jon Samsel. *Interactive Writer's Handbook.* Los Angeles: The Carronade Group, 1995.

Witt, Leonard.(Ed.) *The Complete Book of Feature Writing.* Cincinnati: Writer's Digest Books, 1991.

Index